HOW TO
GIVE YOURSELF
A RAISE
IN SELLING

HOW TO GIVE YOURSELF A RAISE IN SELLING

HOWARD W. BONNELL

BELL PUBLISHING COMPANY
NEW YORK

This 1985 edition is published by Bell Publishing Company, distributed by Crown
Publishers, Inc. by arrangement with Frederick Fell Publishers, Inc.

Printed and bound in the United States of America

Library of Congress Cataloging-in-Publication Data

Bonnell, Howard W.
How to give yourself a raise in selling.

Bibliography: p.
Includes index.
1. Selling. 2. Direct selling. I. Title.
HF5438.25.B65 1985   658.8′5   85-21445
ISBN: 0-517-490072

h g f e d c b a

CONTENTS

FOREWORD

THIS thought often has crossed my mind: "Wouldn't it have been great if, at the start of my selling career, I knew what I know now?" Of course, I can't do it for myself, but I can do it for others. This has inspired me to put into these pages what I learned in 40 years of selling and managing sellers.

To help the reader better understand ideas and techniques in this book, I have used my own sales experience to illustrate where they were applied and how they worked. Some points are repeated for emphasis. I have learned that repetition is a good teacher.

The book is dedicated to those who make selling a career and to those who contemplate selling as a career.

---

* This book is written with the knowledge that both women and men are engaged in the selling profession. Rather than repeating he/she throughout the book, I feel it makes for easier reading to use either he or she. I chose to use he. I trust the women will forgive me.

PREFACE

How to give yourself a raise in selling is a simple, easy-to-read, practical sales book that gives the "hows" and "whys" so critically important to anyone who aspires to a successful career in selling. From the beginning of his book, Howard Bonnell expresses the feelings of many: how they wish they'd had this information before making the first sales call!

Written in a direct yet comprehensive manner, HOW TO GIVE YOURSELF A RAISE IN SELLING will be useful to the person who has never "skinned a knuckle" on a door as well as to the individual who has quit using some of the all-important basics of selling.

Mr. Bonnell writes from a wealth of personal experience. Drawing specifically from "how *he* did it," this book will give you insights into both sales technique and sales psychology. Not only has Howard Bonnell "done it," but he has spent many years successfully teaching others how to sell.

The message of the book is valid as far as technique and procedure are concerned, and is not dependent upon the personality of the sales person. In short, it is a book with a considerable amount of transferable knowledge. Since ideas and knowledge don't care who uses or owns them, the reader will reap the benefits of the many years of trial, effort and error that preceded the author's rise to the top of his chosen profession.

I urge you to read and re-read this book with a pen in your hand, so that you can mark the ideas which best fit your situation. You will also want to make notes in the margins, so that the additional ideas the book engenders can be captured and used in face-to-face encounters with your employer—your customers.

Read it with an enthusiastically open mind, buy the ideas Mr. Bonnell presents, and take them out onto the firing line and put them to work. If you do these things, I *will* SEE YOU AT THE TOP!

ZIG ZIGLAR

INTRODUCTION

WHEN I read a book on salesmanship I am always curious about how the author got started in selling and some of the problems he or she overcame, as well as his or her triumphs. Here is my story.

I lived the first eighteen years of my life in Frankfort, a small town in northeast Kansas. My father operated a large hardware store, as well as a service station and bulk oil business selling to farmers. As a youth I worked for my father. This gave me contact with the salesmen who called on him. I got to know some of them quite well. Their lifestyle intrigued me. They were gregarious, friendly people, and their work enabled them to travel. I considered going into sales because I found it exciting to sell items that particularly appealed to me.

In 1930, I was in college. The Depression was still on, and my father had difficulty keeping his business afloat. After college, my father asked me to help him hold his business together. I agreed, although it meant working for a year for $5 per week plus room and board. After the year, my father felt he could get along without me if I wished to seek my fortune elsewhere.

I had made up my mind to go into sales and sales

management, so I left home and went to Kansas City, Missouri. I finally got a job as a salesman with the largest independent tire dealer in Kansas City. To sell commercial accounts, I was paid $100 per month plus commissions. It didn't take long to find out that I didn't know much about selling, and that no one was going to pay me a salary for a long time to learn. I wanted to get sales training in the direct selling field.

I began by answering an ad in the *Kansas City Star*. The man who interviewed me was recruiting people to sell educational books to parents. I told him I wanted someone to make calls with me and show me how to sell. He answered that any day I wanted to see a sale made, he would make it.

After one week of classroom training, I joined his crew. There were five young people in the crew, and we visited a new town every week. We stayed in rooming houses, not hotels. Lack of success discouraged us all. We joked about this, but the undertone was negative.

After a month, I went back home. I was making payments on a used car, and several times I wrote my father for money. This troubled me because I knew he needed the money for his business. I sat around the house and wallowed in self-pity. Since we lived in a small town everyone knew the situation. My father was a leading businessman and president of the school board, so the Bonnell boys were expected to be successful.

My father wisely let me get the self-pity out of my system, then told me he thought the book business offered me a good opportunity. He gave me $50 and told me to take my car, get away from the negative influence of my associates, and go out and conquer the business world. I did this, and began to have some success. In three months, I was made a manager and had my own crew. Although I had many discouraging times, I managed to get over the starting hurdle.

As the years went by I learned much about myself. Promotions and success came, but it was the struggle that created my strengths. Like all salespeople, I was ready to quit many times. But I knew that quitting would become a habit, and it takes no strength to quit. This background and forty years of working with salespeople struggling to succeed comprise my credentials for writing this book.

HOWARD W. BONNELL

Chapter I

DIRECT SELLING

THE IDEAS and thoughts on selling presented here result from four decades of experience as a salesman. They pertain to all types of selling, and it is my belief that all who read this book will find something to benefit them.

In direct selling, the salesperson deals with an individual who will be using the product personally. This individual might not buy the product or service unless someone calls on him and creates a need and want for it. For instance, the largest business in the world—insurance—got that way because the salespersons went to the prospect.

Even though most people accept the need for insurance, they do not buy enough by initiating the purchase themselves. Rather, an insurance salesperson contacts the person and creates the need and want.

The direct salesperson always will be in great demand, simply because good ones are in short supply. The direct seller works *out of* an office, not *in* an office. He goes to the customer. This requires more planning, self-discipline, and perseverance than is needed by the salesperson who calls on accounts or the one who works in a place of business where customers come preconditioned to make a purchase. The shortage of good, creative direct sellers creates an excellent opportunity for those motivated to be successful.

Advantages of Direct Selling

The demand for direct sellers enables those who are successful to command good incomes and to control their incomes.

They don't have to depend on the customer coming to them. They are limited only by energy, ambition, and selling skills.

Salespeople in stores don't have to knock on doors in all kinds of weather. But their incomes are determined by how many customers come to them. The person who owns the store is the one who earns the big money.

The Service of Selling

Salesmanship is treated as a profession today. Not too long ago, the average seller never read books about the profession. Most people in selling were considered natural-born salespeople. I never subscribed to the theory of the natural-born salesperson. Today, many companies have scientific and professional sales training courses. Their salespeople regularly attend seminars on selling.

One of the things that has given selling a poor image

is people selling things that do not provide the benefits the salespeople claimed for the product.

This is my sales creed: *Selling is a service if what you are selling is a service. If it is not a service and you sell it, you are a hypocrite. If it is a service, you serve only when you sell.*

The United States has one of the highest standards of living of any nation in the world. Mass production usually gets credit for this. But you cannot afford to mass-produce goods unless you can sell what is produced. It is salesmanship that pumps lifeblood into industry and business. As Red Motley, Editor of *Parade Magazine* said, "Nothing happens in this country 'til someone sells something."

People once were suspicious of insurance sellers. They sold nothing for something. Today it's the largest business in the world. The insurance salesperson educated the public to insurance.

The resistance a salesperson experiences to the ideas he tries to sell is normal. People resist change, and especially ideas they don't understand. For example, I grew up in a small town in Kansas where my father ran a large hardware store. In my early teens, I worked in my father's store. I remember farmers talking about the college squirt, the agricultural agent who tried to interest farmers in scientific farming. The agent encountered resistance to ideas he tried to sell. Farmers said, "You don't have to go to college to learn to farm. I was farming when that agent was in knee pants." Today the farmer has finally accepted these ideas to the degree that he sends his sons to agricultural college. The corn didn't used to grow as high as it does now. This is just one example of a good idea that was met with resistance; perhaps there would have been less resistance if the organizational agents had been trained to sell the concepts of scientific farming.

People always resist progress. It means change. People resist things they do not understand. The salesperson's mission is to overcome this resistance, and it can be rewarding.

Choosing Selling as a Career

There are three important factors to consider in making selling a career:

1. The person should decide that selling is what he really wants to do. He should know as much as possible about the benefits of selling, and about the things the profession will require to be successful. Once a person decides benefits outweigh liabilities, he's ready for the second consideration.

2. The salesperson must find a product or service about which he can get excited. He should be certain that if someone purchases the service or product that the person is better off than before the purchase. The product or service should be the best in its field, or at least as good as any other. A salesperson selling a product when he knows his competition has a better one cheats himself and his customer.

3. The seller should select a company having a code of ethics that he can live with. The manner in which the company treats the customer is also the manner in which the company treats its salespeople. A seller should select

a company that is a leader—that is progressive and has a sound sales training program. Other considerations in chosing a company: What is their policy on promotion? Is it based on results? Are there restrictions on earnings? Once a person has satisfied himself about these basic considerations, it is time to go to work.

Creative Selling

Some products require creative selling. They are sold, not bought. Educational books and insurance fall into this category. If the encyclopedia publishers and insurance companies depended on the customer coming to them, they would not be in business long. It is necessary to create a need for the product before it can be sold.

A reporter from *Wall Street Journal* once interviewed a top insurance salesman in Chicago. The salesman said that his job was to talk to fathers about things they didn't want to talk about.

All people have a "want" list. The objective of the sales presentation is to get the product high on the prospect's "want" list.

People Buy What They Want—Not What They Need

Most people buy what they want, not always what they need. All the people that gamble in Las Vegas cannot afford to gamble, but that's what they want to do.

A good technique of selling is to get the prospect to *think* as the salesperson thinks, to *feel* as the salesperson feels, and to *act* as the salesperson wants the prospect to act. Of course, the salesperson must be convinced that getting the prospect to act that way is in the customer's best interest.

How a salesperson feels about the merits of a product is critical. It is often said that a seller must be sold on his product. When a prospect gives the "Can't afford" excuse, further persuasion to buy must be based on the seller's firm conviction that the financial sacrifice which he asks the prospect to make is justified. If the salesperson doesn't feel that way, he should find another product. A salesperson who isn't convinced that the product he sells is as good as any in its field cheats himself and does a disservice to the buyer. If he is convinced that the product renders a service to the prospect that justifies the investment, then the ony way he can serve the prospect is to sell him.

Chapter II

Becoming a
Professional
Salesperson

W HEN Lee Trevino, the golfer, was scheduled to play in a Pro-Am tournament, I decided to watch the contestants tee off. Lee was in a foursome with three company executives. It was revealing to watch Lee and the three executives practice on the putting green. Trevino took many more practice putts than the amateurs. That is why he is a pro. Practice is a self-inflicted discipline that makes a professional in any field.

Some people who want to be salespeople will not accept the discipline required to make them professionals. To become a physician, lawyer, scientist, or engineer, a person must spend years in college. Too many people who go into sales want to reach the same level overnight. They don't have a library, as do professionals in other fields. Yet helpful books and tapes are available in abundance.

The Salesperson's Classroom Is Selling in the Field

Every sales presentation should be a learning experience. This is where a salesperson gets the opportunity to practice and experiment with the ideas and techniques he learns from books, tapes, and successful salespeople.

A salesperson should relive every presentation and try to glean from it something he can use in future presentations. Why did the prospect say what he said? What was the real motive for the prospect's objections? What could the salesperson have said when the objection arose that resulted in the prospect's failure to buy? Was the person a good prospect for the product? Was the demonstration too long, going beyond the prospect's attention span?

Every salesperson should ask himself these and other questions when the presentation is over.

Tape Your Presentation

One of the best ways to improve a presentation is to tape it and then listen to it critically. A tendency exists for salespeople to fill their presentations with too much verbal fat. When listening to the tape, isolate each statement to see if it contributed to the objective of the presentation.

Are You "Telling" or Selling?

In critiquing the presentation, a salesperson should determine if he is merely "telling" a prospect about the product, rather than describing its desirable features and benefits.

Listening to your own presentation reveals how you sound to your prospect. Would you buy from you? Does your presentation come across with conviction, sincerity, and enthusiasm, or does it sound like a recitation?

A good idea is to get a colleague to listen to your presentation while he plays the role of the prospect. If a salesperson makes mistakes in a presentation and does not detect them, every time he gives the presentation he is practicing his mistakes.

There should be few instances when a salesperson feels that a presentation was a total waste of time. At lunch and at the end of the day, relive every presentation to learn how it could have been improved. This procedure makes every presentation a learning experience.

Chapter III

ADJUSTING
TO SALES

I WORK with a company which is in the direct selling field. It is one of the largest in its industry and international in scope. Most of the people selling for this company had no previous sales experience. When interviewed, many of them professed that they didn't think they could sell anything. Most of the people who later became sales managers were the ones who didn't think they could sell well.

People who are not in sales believe that successful sellers have a certain natural quality that marks them as salespeople. If a person doesn't have these qualities, he could never be successful. My experience proves that this theory of the natural-born salesman is a myth.

Time

Someone has said that when a salesman is not in front of a prospect, he's unemployed.

There are so many ways salesmen waste valuable time. A few of these time wasters are: coffee breaks, back-tracking because the calls are not organized geographically, stopping to make deposits in the bank rather than by mail, taking the children to school, getting started half an hour late, quitting half an hour early, doing paperwork in prime selling hours, staying too long with non-prospects, talking to non-prospects, talking to non-decision makers.

If by better utilization of time a salesperson could get in an extra sales presentation a day, it would result in a great raise in income.

Each salesperson should do a time-and-motion study on himself to see how much of his average day is spent in front of a prospect. The results may be surprising, but they will certainly help in developing a system for greater productivity.

Self-Discipline

Where does one get self-discipline? Certainly, we don't inherit it from our parents. Self-discipline must be developed. If a salesperson desires to achieve his goals and he is strong enough, he will eventually develop self-discipline.

There are several things a person can do to make it a bit easier doing the things one should do rather than the things one wants to do. For instance, getting started in the morning is always difficult. It is more difficult if the evening before the salesperson has not committed himself to a definite starting time and place.

I discovered that if I spent the last half-hour of my day inquiring or prospecting and then made a commitment to be at the prospect's door at 9 A.M., it made it easier for me to get started the next morning. If, however, I got up in the morning and said, "I wonder where I should work today," I found that I had a tendency to procrastinate and find excuses to avoid what I knew I should be doing.

A salesperson, to be successful, needs self-discipline. The 1,100 people in our office show up each working day on time. They are not on time because they possess more self-discipline than people in sales. These people are paid a salary and lateness and absenteeism are not tolerated. In essence, the company is providing the discipline.

A new salesperson, who in previous jobs didn't need self-discipline, now finds it absolutely necessary. When will he make the first call? Who will he call on? If he makes the wrong choice too often, he won't be in sales long.

Structuring Work

In many sales positions the salesperson is left to his own devices. When he first becomes a salesperson he suddenly finds himself in a position where he is offered options he has never experienced. In his sales positions he may not be required to show up at an office, so the burden of his being on the job is is placed on the salesperson. Never before has he had this choice. So thoughts like—Where will I work today? When should I get started? Who will I call on?—enter his mind. Having no previous commitment and the intangible uncertainties as to when, where, and who to call on contributes to his tendency to procrastinate and to operate inefficiently.

In the salesperson's previous position his assignments were clear, precise, and very tangible. Now, however, the burden of these decisions and commitments are placed squarely on his shoulders. He must create something that doesn't exist, and if his manager fails to provide structuring, then the burden is upon the salesperson to structure himself. Most people cannot handle unstructured work.

I have often had sales representatives who had been teachers say to me, "When I was teaching I knew when my day began, where I was to be each hour, and what I would be doing. In selling there is not enough structure for me to feel secure. I need to be committed to some definite activity."

Intangibles

Early in the salesperson's career, what to do and the anticipated rewards can be quite intangible. This may add to the new seller's feeling of insecurity.

Mental Attitude

Positive thoughts produce positive results. This law works in reverse. I am convinced that a salesperson's mental attitude is an 85 percent factor in his success as a salesperson. The salesperson must learn to have faith in the law of averages. This is dealt with in detail later in this book.

Good Days / Bad Days

In a previous job, the new salesperson may not have experienced good days and bad days. Perhaps he rarely went home at night discouraged, wondering if he would make any money the next day. In his sales work now there may be no salary. If a seller is on a straight commission, he gets paid only when he sells.

Rejection

I have interviewed people for sales positions and they said, "I couldn't sell. I can't ask people for money. If the customer came to me, then I would enjoy selling."

What these people are really saying is, I can't stand rejection. I have to be loved. People who feel this way often suffer from low self-esteem. Their ego nerve ends have been frayed and they would interpret the prospect's refusal to buy the product as a personal rejection.

Occasionally when making calls with a new representative, we might call on a prospect who seems irritated about our calling and states she wouldn't be interested, and closes the door. To my new sales representative, this can be devastating. He feels totally rejected and shot down.

Generally, to modify and lessen the impact of this experience, I will suggest we go out in the car and discuss it. I will point out to the representative that we were tactful and diplomatic in approaching the prospect and she didn't respond in kind, so that person has a problem. I will also

point out to the new representative that in all probability
the prospect is really a nice person, but she may have been
up all night with a sick child, or she might have had a fight
with her husband that morning. That woman wanted to
lower the boom on someone, and we were the first candi-
dates who came along. I remind the salesperson that it's
terrific we don't have to work with that person all day.
Then I say, "Let's call on our next prospect, who probably
doesn't have this problem."

This is the rationale that a salesperson must learn to
accept if he is going to overcome the concern about rejection.

Fluctuating Income

Most workers get a paycheck for the same amount
every week or every two weeks. They can count on this.
This gives them a feeling of security and stability. In a
sales job, this may not be true. But there is the potential
for greater income and achievement. The more you sell,
the more you get paid.

Fear of Failure

Before getting into sales, a person may have been free
of fear of failure. Now, as a salesperson, this fear has to
be coped with. Learning to make adjustments is critical.
I've seen people with obvious talents for selling fail or quit

because they could not make these adjustments.

Influence of the Spouse

When interviewing a person to join our company, we always include the spouse. We know he or she will have more influence on the new salesperson than we will have. The spouse must be 100 percent in favor of his or her partner joining the company or we do not hire the person. If the spouse does not support the salesperson, he or she will fail.

All these adjustments will be dealt with in more detail later.

Chapter IV

USING
BODY LANGUAGE
IN SELLING

W E ALL use body language, although most people are not aware of it. Body language includes facial expressions, gestures, the way we sit, the way we stand.

One of the most important things to do when meeting a prospect for the first time is to put him at ease. This can be done in several ways, but body language is one of the most important. The salesperson should appear relaxed. He shouldn't slump in his chair, but appear to be completely at ease. Leaning back in the chair with your arms resting comfortably will help a prospect to relax. If you appear nervous, tense, or aggressive, the prospect feels ill at ease or threatened.

Action does speak louder than words. For instance, hand someone a pencil and usually he or she takes it without you having to say a word. As another example, assume you are in your home with a friend. His coat is on the back of the chair and the two of you are conversing. There is a movie you would like to see and you want your friend to go with you. You could use one of the two approaches to persuade him to go:

APPROACH NO. 1: You simply say, "Bill, there is a great movie in town I've been wanting to see. How about going with me?"

APPROACH NO. 2: You get up and hold his coat while you say, "Bill, there's a great movie I've been wanting to see, let's go see it together."

If Bill is totally uninterested in seeing the movie, he will decline. However, if he is at all receptive to the idea, he will probably go without too much thought, because Approach No. 2 relieves him of the burden of deciding. All he has to do is follow your suggestion. The next time you go to a crowded theatre or sporting event, try this: Look down (body language) and say "Pardon me." Those in front of you will move out of your way, because lack of eye contact with those you are trying to pass eliminates a possible rebuff.

When a Customer Objects

When a prospect responds to your close with an excuse, it is important that you not allow him to think you are concerned about the excuse. You do this by sitting back, appearing relaxed and dealing with the excuse. If a prospect sees that the excuse has impact on you, he will continue to use that excuse.

Body Language When Closing

When closing, you should start writing on an order pad as you ask for the order. This action creates the assumption that the prospect is going to buy. It is easier for him to follow than to lead. The closing statement is usually an optional choice. The choice might be between one color or another, supported by the body language of the order pad and pen poised to write. It will result in the order if the prospect has been brought to the point where he is seriously considering buying.

Prospect's Body Language

Watch the prospect's body language to determine how close he is to buying. Eyes, gestures, comments, responses, and questions all indicate interest or lack of it. A smart salesperson watches and listens to the signals the prospect unconsciously gives to show how he really feels about buying.

Chapter V

EXPLAINING
VERSUS SELLING

IN THE early months of my sales career, the objective of my presentation was to convince the prospect that I had the finest product of its kind. Usually I succeeded in doing this. But when I tried to close, the prospects would say: "That's the finest set of books we've seen, but we can't afford it."

Further training and a better understanding of salesmanship made me realize that I was explaining the product in detail. As a result, the prospect respected the product, but didn't want it badly enough to buy it.

There are many things I respect that I don't want to own. I respect the elephant. It is the largest beast of burden; it has a fantastic memory, and I like to watch it perform in a circus. But I never developed a desire to own one.

I made the mistake of telling the prospect about the product, instead of telling him or her what it would do for the family that they wanted done for the family. Describing a product doesn't make the prospect want it. What the product will do for him is what makes him want it.

If a person studies TV commercials, he can see they are designed to sell benefits. I remember a commercial for the deodorant Ice Blue Secret. The opening scene shows two girls living together in a college dormitory. Mary seems upset about something.

Her roommate says, "Mary, you seem upset. What's the matter?" Mary replies that she has a date for the big college dance, and she is afraid that she won't smell nice. (Well, it didn't come off quite that crudely, but that was implied.) Mary's roommate says, "Don't worry, I have the answer." The next scene shows the roommate holding a can of Ice Blue Secret. She assures Mary that using it will keep Mary cool all evening. Mary appears more relaxed when she has this protection going for her. The final scene shows Mary coming in at five A.M. The dance was over at midnight she tells her roommate, but her date kept her out until he proposed marriage. Now, you can't beat that for benefits.

The commercial doesn't describe what is in Ice Blue Secret. Any young girl watching the commercial doesn't care about that if the product will do for her what it did for Mary. That's what makes the girls want it.

The professional, creative salesperson points out the features of the product, but he also describes what each feature will do for the prospect.

Emotional Appeal

Dale Carnegie said, "When dealing with people, remember you are not dealing with creatures of logic, but with creatures of emotions, creatures bristling with prejudice and motivated by pride and vanity.''

People are motivated more by emotions than by logic. A woman will suffer the discomfort of a girdle all day, or a man will put up with a tie or a toupé, because they look better.

Some products possess more emotional appeal than others. Generally, those in the equipment or strictly commercial lines are not emotionally motivated purchases. However, those sold for personal use such as cars, jewelry, cosmetics, clothes, insurance and educational books have emotional appeal. The salesperson can exploit this appeal.

An automobile is an emotionally motivated purchase. Certainly a car is essential today, but the motive to get a new one is primarily emotional. The only difference between two men looking at new models in an auto showroom and two boys looking at new toys in a toy store is ages. Here is an example: Frank loves cars. He brags about his own which has 25,000 miles on it and uses no oil. One day Frank is mowing his lawn when a new red convertible with a white top parks in front of his house. Frank recognizes the driver as one of his neighbors.

The neighbor waves to Frank to come and see the car. ''How do you like my new car?'' he asks. Frank congratulates him with all the false enthusiasm he can muster because he is jealous. The neighbor says, ''Get in and drive this baby.'' Frank, reluctantly, gets behind the wheel, puts the car in gear, and steps on the gas pedal. The car takes off so fast that Frank nearly hit another car. It has much more power than his own car. He drives the car around the block and parks it. Again, he congratulates his friend. His neighbor parks the car in his driveway where Frank can see it.

The want for a new car is planted. Frank doesn't need one, but he wants a new car and the want is never going to go away. How can he justify doing this if he has been bragging about how great his present car is? Frank starts looking for logical reasons to satisfy an emotional urge.

About a month later Frank comes home with this story to his wife. " You know, honey, I had a flat tire going to work this morning. It's getting so that I can't depend on that car. [Hear the logic ?] I was late for work and the boss didn't like it. On the way home I stopped by the tire store to have the tire fixed. I decided to have them check all the tires because we have the vacation trip coming up this summer, and I wouldn't want the kids riding in an unsafe car. [Frank's always thinking of the children.] The tires are pretty worn, so I asked the clerk what it would cost to put the best tires on the car." [Frank isn't interested in new tires, that is why he asked the price of the *best* tires.] Frank now tells his wife that new tires cost $200.00, and that he has been hearing disturbing noises in the backend. Besides, it doesn't have much power any more. He tells her that he doesn't think it is wise to put all that money in the old car, so he is going to look for a new one.

That is an example of how people sell themselves on buying new cars. The automobile industry understands how to get people to trade in their cars for the new models— they change the outside appearance each year. Dress and suit manufacturers do the same thing with women's and men's clothing.

To sell successfully, you must understand what motivates people to want things. If your product makes the prospect look better, benefits her children, protects his family, enhances her image, or makes life easier, you have powerful appeal for your product.

Chapter VI

THE
SALES
PRESENTATION

W ORDS are the salesperson's tools. Selection of the right words is critical.

Two shoe shops hung signs over their doors. One read: "Shoes Fixed While You *Wait*." The other read: "Shoes Fixed While You *Rest*." Changing one word makes the message more appealing. Waiting conveys no benefit, but rest does.

Writers and speakers choose words close to their thoughts. The result, as Dr. French says in his treatise, *On The Study Of Words:* "Will not be too big here, hanging like a giant's robe on the limbs of dwarf; nor too small there, as a boy's garments into which a man has painfully and ridiculously thrust himself."

I have some words I have eliminated from my sales vocabulary. One of these is "decision." People don't like to make decisions. "Choices" are more appealing.

Most people believe that selling involves lots of talking. You have heard people say, "He's a good salesman; he has a good gift of gab." Nothing could be further from the truth. Good sellers get ideas across with an economy of words. Adults have attention and listening spans, just as children do.When a salesperson goes beyond this span, he ends up being the only one listening.

You should refine your description of a product, its features and its benefits to eliminate unnecessary words. One good way to do this is to record your presentation on tape. Then listen to determine what words are not necessary to express the thoughts or concepts you want to convey.

When demonstrating the *World Book Encyclopedia,* our company emphasizes to parents the importance of being able to answer their children's questions. We sell this idea with a humorous story. I will tell the story in two ways.

"Mr. Prospect, you may have heard the story about the little boy who was playing outside. A question popped into his mind, and he came into the house and went up to his father for an answer. The father was reading the paper. He put down the paper and said, 'Johnny, I'm sorry, I don't know the answer to your question.'

"The little boy was disappointed and went out to play. Soon he had another question that he wanted answered. He returned to the house and asked his father. Again, the father put down the paper and admitted he didn't know the answer. The boy went back to playing again, and a third question came to his mind. He went back into the house and again approached his father for an answer. The father admitted again that he couldn't answer his son's question.

"The little boy said, 'Dad, I hope you don't mind me asking you these questions.'

"The father replied, 'That's all right son, how else are you going to learn.' "

If you eliminate unnecessary words, the same point can be made with this version.

"Mr. Prospect, you may have heard the story about the little boy who was playing in the yard.

"A question popped into his mind, so he came into the house and asked his father the question. The father confessed that he didn't know the answer.

"A little while later the boy was back again with another question, and he got the same response. Pretty soon he was back with a third question with the same results.

"The little boy said to his father, 'I hope you don't mind me pestering you with these questions.' The father replied, 'That's all right, son, how else are you going to learn.' "

The first story took 169 words. The second took 107 words. The second telling was just as effective in getting the point across.

Prospects often have a limited amount of time to listen to a sales presentation. This is another reason for cutting out unnecessary words.

A tendency exists, particularly for new salespeople, to adlib to keep the interview going. This usually involves what I call "verbal garbage" or "fat." When "fat" becomes part of a presentation, the presentation may get longer and longer. Statements such as, "Isn't it attractive, beautiful, outstanding," etc., mean little. A salesperson should be concrete and precise.

Sir Arthur Quilter Couch puts it this way in his book, *On The Art Of Writing:* "So long as you prefer abstract words which express other men's summarized concepts of things, to concrete ones which lie as near as can be reached to things themselves and are first-hand material for your thoughts, you will remain, at the best, writers at second-hand."

As an experiment, record on tape the words you use to describe a feature and its benefits. Transfer the words to paper, then see which ones you can eliminate and still get the concept across. This exercise should remove superfluous and unnecessary words and reduce the time a prospect has to listen.

In designing a presentation, avoid general statements that do not carry authority. Instead of "Isn't it attractive" or "Isn't it beautiful," say "Research shows that," "Educators tell us," "Authorities say." The more authoritative a statement, the more believable it is to the prospect. However, a salesperson should be certain he or she is on solid ground when they make a claim.

What if Winston Churchill said something like this: "Now, I may be wrong about this, but it would be my suggestion that we fight them on the beaches. I also feel we should engage them on the landing grounds, and in the fields and streets, if necessary. There is a possibility we may fight them even in the hills. Some of you may not agree with me, but, if I have it my way, we shall never surrender."

Eliminate the "I"

A presentation is weakened by statements such as, "I think this," "I believe this," etc.

A prospect is interested, not in the opinions of salespeople, but in facts or statements by authorities related to the needs the product serves. In this regard, testimonials of product owners carry weight.

You don't have to be an authority, or represent yourself as one. Instead, you should represent those who are authorities in the particular field that the product is designed to serve.

Dramatization

A professional salesperson masters the art of dramatization. You should think of yourself as being on the stage during your presentation. Some people refer to this as "romancing" a product.

A whisper can be as dramatic as a scream. Enthusiasm should be conveyed by tone of voice. A monotone will put the prospect to sleep.

Too many salespeople do not consider how words should sound. Some salespeople say "success" and "failure" with the same facial expression and the same voice inflection. Success is better than failure; don't make them sound the same. Use your voice, facial expressions, visual aids, a prospectus, and the product to bring life and meaning to your words.

Here is a test and practice presentation to see if you can "romance" a lead pencil. Remember—point to the features as you tell about the product:

> Forget laundry bills. This pre-tested, chrome yellow, hard-finished writing instrument positively will not leak. It keeps your hands free of ink and your clothes soft and spotless. This pencil is fabricated from the finest second-growth hickory. It is graphite-filled with fine-grained jet-black carbon which cannot snag or catch on any paper surface. It writes in any weather. You don't have to refill it, and it is inexpensive enough to discard when completely used. It fits standard sharpeners and has no unsightly pocket clip. I'm sure you want one, don't you?

Practice this exercise to see if you can make an ordinary pencil a thing to desire.

A salesperson should ask: "Do my prospects think I like my product, or do they think I'm in love with it?" He or she should use gestures, facial expressions, and posture to convey enthusiasm and conviction when discussing the features and benefits of the product. Give your sales presentation in a mirror. Then answer the question: "Would you buy from you?"

A story is told about a young clerk employed in a jewelry store. A lady came in to look at a diamond ring. The clerk selected a ring from the display case and described the beauty and art of the diamond. When the customer asked the price, the clerk answered, "$5,000." Shocked at the price, the customer decided against buying.

The owner of the store then stepped up to the counter,

picked up the ring and placed it on a black velvet pad. He began to extol the quality of the ring in an eloquent manner and the customer bought it. The young clerk was astonished and surprised. The store owner told the young clerk: "The problem is you like diamonds, but I am in love with them."

We often hear the statement that a person should be sold on the product he sells. Even more, a salesperson should have a missionary zeal for his product. Too many people sell products for which they have no deep feeling. Finding the right product that you feel in your heart will bring needed benefits to the prospect is critical.

True conviction and sincerity will be recognized, as will lack of true conviction and sincerity.

Strong convictions regarding the benefits of the product will give a salesperson the will to persuade the prospect to buy in spite of his objections. The salesperson must feel in his own heart that such persuasion serves the best interest of the prospect. If you find yourself in front of a prospect and realize your product will not serve that person's needs, you should graciously leave and find someone who truly needs the product.

Tempo

People can listen to 690 words per minute comfortably. If you speak distinctly, you need not concern yourself about talking too rapidly. On the other hand, you can train yourself to talk distinctly *and* rapidly. I have trained myself to talk rapidly because I want the prospect to feel the excitement I feel about the product. Rapid speech and excitement go hand-in-hand. However, you cannot give your entire presentation at the same speed. Slowing down for emphasis and for change of pace makes the presentation more interesting.

Stories and Analogies

Stories and analogies are excellent for getting across ideas and concepts to the prospect. Christ used parables for this purpose. The Bible is full of them. Well-told stories capture a prospect's interest and attention and inject a change of pace in the sales presentation.

Humor

Humor is a valuable tool if the salesperson has the ability to use it. Two people laughing together are not too far apart.

Humor is especially valuable in the warm-up part of a presentation when you try to develop rapport with the prospect. It relieves the prospect's anxieties about how he is going to be treated.

Humor can also lessen the impact on an objection.

Ascertain early in the presentation if your prospect has a sense of humor. This will guide you in determining how much humor to use, and how it will be received.

Memorize the Presentation

The difference between an amateur and a professional is embodied in his or her performance. The actual performance of a professional involves conditioned reflexes. For example, a golf pro doesn't think about gripping a club. The grip is a preconditioned, automatic reflex. This frees the pro to think about how he is going to get the ball where he wants it to go.

When learning to drive a stick-shift automobile the beginner concentrates on the correct procedure of shifting gears. Once he or she learns to drive, shifting becomes a subconscious reflex, freeing the driver to concentrate on steering the car. The same is true with selling. The features of most products lend themselves to standardized presentation. I have heard people say that they do not believe this, because prospects vary widely. I agree that a salesperson must tailor the presentation to the personality, interests, education, wants, and needs of the prospect. However, every successful seller has evolved a certain standardized presentation. Through trial and error, they have discovered that certain words enable them to describe the features of the product most effectively and to relate those features to the perceived needs of the prospect. With time-tested phraseology, the salesperson does not grope for words. He or she perfects the presentation by using the proper voice inflection, modulation, and dramatization, and is confident about the results.

Those people who are opposed to "canned" presentations don't know what they are talking about. The trouble with most "canned" presentations is that they aren't "canned" well enough. Half-canned presentations sound like Johnnie in front of the class trying to recite the poem he hasn't quite memorized. The professional with a presentation well-planted in his subconscious mind frees his conscious mind to study the prospect and the amount of interest his presentation is having on the prospect. His standardization includes strategies that he can match to an individual and the amount of interest displayed. An effective salesperson listens to the prospect and evaluates what his words may reveal about the prospect's concerns, problems, and objections. This clues the salesperson to what standard techniques should be employed.

A sales presentation is like a speech or play. A professional public speaker, or an actor, must master the presentation to hold the attention of the audience.

Chapter VII

CLOSING
THE SALE

A SALESMAN selling meat-slicing machines called on a butcher in a small town several times, but he could not persuade the old butcher to let him demonstrate the machine. The butcher argued that he could slice meat by hand and didn't need an expensive machine.

One day the salesman was in the butcher's town, and he decided to make one last effort. The butcher finally agreed to let him demonstrate the machine. As the salesman did this, he asked the butcher, "Doesn't this machine cut slices more evenly than by hand?" The butcher agreed. The salesman noted that the machine would save waste. The butcher agreed. Exasperated, the salesman said, "Then why don't you buy this machine?" The butcher replied, "You didn't ask me."

This story illustrates one of the most difficult techniques you must learn to apply if you are to be a great salesperson. What keeps salespeople from asking for the order? The answer is fear of an objection. These objections can be interpreted in many ways by the salesperson.

Rejection

A salesperson can interpret a "no" or an excuse as a personal rejection. This may indicate that the salesperson has a self-image problem. His ego nerve-ends are exposed. Some people are supersensitive to rejection, probably due to child/parent relationship during their formative years.

Children criticized and not given much approval by their parents often are sensitive to rejection as adults. This does not mean that they cannot change, but changing personality is not easy or rapid.

"No" Means No?

The inexperienced salesperson feels that "no" means no, or termination of the sales demonstration. The experienced salesperson learns that a "no" and excuses not to buy are not necessarily final. The best way to learn this is to get some sales after a prospect has objected several times, or to see a professional salesperson overcome excuses and get the order.

Two Wills Opposing Each Other

Everyone has sales resistance. Such resistance stems from many factors. Some people have had bad experiences with salespeople. If a person has suffered from buyer's remorse, he or she will resist salespeople. Also, it feels safer not to buy. Most people do not like to make decisions or commitments, so they resist, even though they want the product.

In every sales demonstration, two wills oppose each other: the salesperson's will to persuade and the customer's will to resist. The will that weakens first strengthens the other.

When my son was five or six years old, he often came along when I went to the drugstore. While I was at the counter, he would come up to me with a bag of candy. Here's how the conversation would go:

> Son: "Daddy, will you buy me this candy?" (Close No. 1)
> Me: "No, son, put the candy back." (Excuse No. 1)
> Son: "But, Daddy, this is my favorite candy; please get me this candy." (Close No. 2)

I felt that I must be strong with my objection to convince him that he could not get the candy.

> Me: "No, son, no candy. Put it back." (Excuse No. 2)
> Son: "Daddy, if you will get me this candy, I'll not ask for any candy for a week." (Close No. 3)
> Me: "I really don't think you need the candy." (Excuse No. 3)

At this point, my modified excuse indicates to my son that my will has weakened. Knowing this, his will is strengthened. If my son had responded to one of my excuses in a manner that indicated he didn't think he was going to get the candy, my will to resist him would be strengthened. I would be encouraged to persist in efforts to dissuade him. From this dialogue you might remember incidents when you were persuaded by a member of your family to do something to which you appeared strongly opposed.

The Will to Persuade

How does an honest salesperson get the will to persuade the prospect to buy a product when the prospect says that he can't afford it? Is a salesperson justified in continuing the presentation when the prospect says that he wants to think it over, or he can't afford it? You are justified if you are convinced that the benefits the prospect will derive are worth the cost of the product. For this to be the case, you must be sold on the product yourself.

A salesperson doesn't serve prospects unless he sells them. If the salesperson becomes convinced of the validity of the prospect's excuses or objections, he should terminate the interview.

Objection Does Not Mean Termination

Some salespeople feel that an excuse not to buy means the interview is over. The professional salesperson believes it is just beginning.

Company records show that 70 percent of our sales are made after the prospect has given three objections to buying. This proves these objections were excuses. The prospect really was saying,"You haven't sold me yet."

The prospect keeps a mental scale in his/her mind. At the time a salesperson calls the prospect's dollars outweigh his/her want and need for the product. As the salesperson demonstrates features and benefits of the product, the prospect's mental scale should move in favor of it. The salesperson makes the first close to determine: (1) What is the excuse, if any, and (2) How near is the prospect to buying? (Is the scale in balance?) An excuse at this point is to be expected. The salesperson agrees with the prospect ("I understand how you feel"), but continues to demonstrate additonal features and benefits.

The salesperson then closes the second time. If the prospect's scale is not balanced, he/she will give another objection. The professional salesperson listens to determine if the prospect has modified his/her objection. If he/she has, this tells the salesperson that he is bringing the prospect closer to buying (the scale is coming into balance).

Again, the salesperson appears to agree, but he directs the attention of the prospect to additional features and benefits.

If, on the third close, the prospect's excuse appears weaker, it indicates that he/she is on the verge of buying. The salesperson creates more want, more benefits, then closes a fourth time. He works until the scale balances and the prospect buys.

DIAGRAM OF A SALE

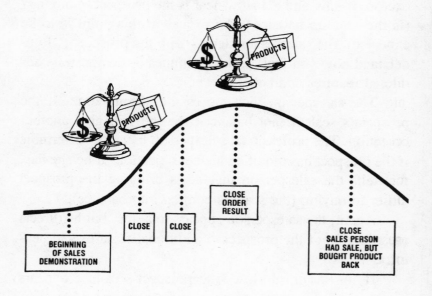

Unmodified Objections

When a prospect's third object is as adamant as the first, you must use your best emotional and logical answer. Then proceed to show more features and benefits, and close again. If the excuse remains firm, it may result in a no-sale.

Two Ways to Bring the Scale into Balance

As I have discussed previously, the objective of the sales presentation is to bring the prospect's mental scale into balance.

One way is to place more need use and value on product side of the scale.

Another method is to lighten the dollar side of the scale. This can be done by reducing the investment or cost to the ridiculous.

In selling *World Book* to a prospect, I might hand the prospect a piece of paper and ask him to do some figuring for me. Here's how the conversation would go:

"Mr. Prospect, would you write down on that paper $399 [the price of *World Book*]. Now your family would get maximum use from it for ten years, so divide the $399 by ten." [After he has done this, say], "How much does that come to?"

Prospect: "$39.90."

Me: "That's correct, you could provide the educational benefits of *World Book* to your children for $39.90

a year. Now divide that amount by two, because both your children will be benefiting from it. What does that come to?''

Prospect: "That comes to $19.95."

Me: "It means that each of your children will get the benefits of *World Book* at a cost to you of only $19.95 per child per year. Now let's divide the $19.95 by 52 weeks to see what it will cost per week per child."

Prospect: "Thirty-eight cents."

Me: "Correct, this means you will be investing only thirty-eight cents per week for each of your children. Surely, the benefits to them are worth thirty-eight cents a week. That is less than the cost of two Cokes a week. Don't you agree that's a good value?"

This technique lightens the dollar side of the scale and reduces the cost to the ridiculous.

Why Not Close Once?

Inexperienced salespeople often ask: "Why not show all features, create the maximum benefit, then close at the right psychological time?" The problem is that, by not closing and eliciting responses, a salesperson remains in the dark about how near the prospect's scale is to being balanced. If a salesperson talks too long, the scale could become unbalanced again in favor of the prospect's money. This is why some people sell their prospects, then they buy the product back again.

The prospect's objection in response to the salesperson's close may indicate that the prospect is resisting making a decision to buy. It does not necessarily mean that he has closed his mind to buying. Once, however, the prospect has made up his mind not to buy, rarely will he/she be sold on that sales presentation. If the salesperson attempts to demonstrate every feature and benefit to create the maximum need and want, and close, he runs the risk of closing after the prospect has decided not to buy.

Do Not Modify the Assumptive Close

There are several closing techniques. Most professional salespeople use the assumptive subordinate choice close. This approach assumes that the prospect is going to buy the product, so all the salesperson does is offer choices. For example: "Would you prefer the white model or the black model?" or "Would you prefer the first payment to come due in 30 days, or would 45 days be better?"

The third closing should be as assumptive as the first. The prospect listens and if the third closing is less assumptive, he/she sees the salesperson's confidence declining. When this happens the prospect feels that the salesperson agrees with his/her objections, and the sale is lost.

Provide Leadership

When a salesperson properly assumes the sale, his attitude says: "I am so confident you see the benefits, as I do, that I am sure you will want my product." When the prospect's mental scale could be influenced either way, the salesperson's closing provides the leadership that tips the scale in favor of the product.

As a salesperson, I enjoy observing the techniques of people who try to sell me. Once I went into a shoe store during the noon hour, thinking I needed a new pair of shoes. The clerk asked me the size, color, and style of shoe I had in mind, then he brought out several pairs. I tried them on and finally returned to the first pair. If the shoe clerk had been a salesperson, he would have sensed that the shoes I tried on the second time were the ones that interested me. I sat there trying to decide what to do.

It should have been obvious to him that my mental scale was in balance. I could have been influenced either way. To consummate that sale all he had to do was assume that I was going to buy. He could have done so by picking up the shoe box (body language) and saying, "Mr. Bonnell, would you like to wear the new shoes? I can put your old ones in this box and wrap them up for you."

At that point, I would have purchased the shoes. Instead, the clerk let me sit there struggling with indecision. This gave me time to think maybe I ought to look around. I didn't have to make a decision that day. So I didn't. That clerk lost the sale to another store. He has probably lost thousands of sales that way. If he had led me, I would have followed. Instead, he placed the burden of decision on me. He wouldn't help me.

How to Tell if the Scale Is Coming into Balance

As mentioned previously, multiple closes will, in most instances, reveal the salesperson's progress in bringing the scale into balance. There are other techniques that can be used, such as clincher questions. These are statements ending in a question. For example: "Mr. Prospect, you can see how this widget will save you time, can't you?" Responses to clinchers provide clues about the progress made towards convincing a prospect.

Salespeople must listen as well as talk. By listening to the prospect you can determine if the response to the clincher question has any conviction or sincerity.

The salesperson needs to know if he is selling and if the prospect is buying. If no progress is being made toward bringing the mental scale into balance, perhaps the salesperson does not have a bonafide prospect.

Close Early and Often

A professional salesperson closes early and often. There are several reasons for this:

1. The salesperson wants the prospect to give the excuse while he/she still has benefits and features to show.

2. The prospect may not actually get involved in the buying process until he/she has voiced the excuse. The sooner this happens, the better.

3. The salesperson wants to plant the seed of potential ownership early in the presentation. The sooner this is

done, the sooner the prospect gets accustomed to the idea.

4. The salesperson wants to see if the second excuse is as adamant and serious as the first. This is why salespeople must be good listeners.

Test Questions

A salesperson should use every technique to find out how close the prospect is to making a favorable decision. Test questions can be used to get this feedback, such as: "In what room would you install this unit?" "Which of the three colors appeals to you?" "How long have you thought about getting more coverage, a new car, etc.?" "If you provide this for your family, would you buy on the easy payment plan, or would you pay cash?"

Answers to such questions should provide clues to how close the prospect is to a decision.

How to Determine if Closing Is Assumptive

When using the choice-question technique, closing is assumptive if it results in either an objection or an agreement to buy. If neither happens, the prospect does not feel that he/she was offered a choice. When employing this technique, the prospect should be made to feel that there are two distinct choices. A correct way to present choices would be to say: "Mr. Prospect, would you prefer your first monthly payment to begin 30 days from today, or would 45 days be better?''

The wrong way to present choices would be to say: "Mr. Prospect, would you prefer the first monthly payment to begin in 30 days or 45 days?'' This example does not include the words "or would.'' The two words "or would'' makes two distinct choices. Without them, it sounds like only one choice.

If a closing does not result in either an agreement to buy or an objection, the value of the close is lost.

Body Language While Closing

When the salesperson closes with the choice questions, body language strengthens the assumption that the prospect will buy. The salesperson should have an order pad out as the closing questions are asked, or right after they have been offered. The salesperson looks down, breaking eye contact with the prospect, and has his pen poised to write.

If the Closing Results in an Objection

No harm is done. In fact, the progress has been made provided these conditions exist:

1. The salesperson has ability to create need and want for the product.
2. The prospect is a bonafide one.

When a salesperson assumes tactfully that the person is going to buy, he demonstrates firm conviction that the prospect should and will appreciate benefits the product will bring.

This technique also creates the impression that everyone is buying. To illustrate this point, assume that a salesperson is making his first presentation. He has the prospect sold, ready to sign the order. If the salesperson says, "Mr. Prospect, you are the first person to buy this product in this town," the prospect may have second thoughts about buying.

The salesperson should create the impression that if the prospect doesn't buy, he would be surprised. The way to get a person to do what you want him/her to do is to assume he/she is going to do it.

Assuming High Pressure

Some salespeople fear that assuming the sale gives the impression of high pressure. Let me use another example to dispel this idea. I have a piece of candy, and I say to you:

> Me: "Do you like candy?" (Clincher)
> You: "Yes, I do." (Agreement)
> Me: "Do you like candy with nuts?" (Clincher)
> You: "Yes, I like nuts." (Agreement)
> Me: "Do you like candy with caramel?" (Clincher)
> You: "I sure do." (Agreement)
> Me: "How about chocolate on the outside, do you like

that?''(Clincher)
You: "Yes, I love chocolate.'' (Agreement)

I have mentioned the features and benefits of the candy, and you have agreed to the benefits. Would I be presumptious in handing you the candy and saying,''Here, have this candy?''

I'm sure you agree that this is not presumptious. In fact, you would be surprised if I didn't expect you to take this candy. If, however, you said you didn't like nuts, hated caramel, and despised chocolate, I would have no right to assume you wanted the candy.

If a prospect agrees to the value of the product's features, it is consistent to assume the prospect wants the product and the benefits it brings. But suppose a salesperson describes the features of the candy, gets your agreement, then says, "Would you like this candy?'' The prospect might be surprised and doubts might creep into his/her mind as to whether he/she wanted it or not. He/she might think there is something wrong with the candy.

You will get some orders by not closing. However, you will get many more by leading the prospect in this way. The salesperson who periodically closes during his demonstration is making it easier for the prospect to buy. Thus more orders result.

Validity of the Excuse

A professional salesperson knows that a ''no'' to a

closing does not mean a sale will not result. He has sold many people after they have given several excuses for not buying.

Let's consider what an excuse could mean. Assume the prospect's response on the first close was: "I can't afford to buy now." The prospect really may be saying: (1) "You haven't convinced me it's worth the money." (2) "I don't buy the first time a salesperson asks me to buy. I want to object first." (3) "I am not interested enough in your product to buy it; there are other things I want to buy more." (4) "It looks good, but I am not sure I want to buy. Show me more."

The salesperson has no way of knowing which of the above is correct. But if he continues to sell benefits and create a desire to buy, the excuses become less adamant. This tells a salesperson that the prospect's mental scale is balancing in favor of the product.

If excuses after subsequent closes do not weaken, the Number 3 condition exists, or financial conditions actually do prevent the prospect from buying. The multiple-closing technique, however, will enable the salesperson to overcome excuses if conditions Number 1, 2, or 4 exist.

Probing Questions

A salesperson can test the validity of an excuse by repeating it and waiting for the prospect to elaborate.

Prospect: "I don't think we can afford to buy now."

Salesperson (with a smile): "You don't think you can afford to buy now?"

The salesperson then waits for the prospect to explain. This may reveal a valid reason for the excuse, or it may indicate that the object can be overcome.

In most instances, the objection is not valid. The salesperson must probe to find the real reason. He must treat any objection as an excuse unless he learns that an objection is real and he must deal with it. If the salesperson shows concern about the excuse early in the presentation, he may contribute to the prospect's feeling about its validity.

That is why an excuse should be treated by a statement such as: "I can see why you would feel that way, but let me show you how this next feature will benefit you."

Ways Salespeople Show Concern Over Excuses

A salesperson exhibits concern over the excuse when he (1) shows disappointment on his face; (2) allows a pause before he agrees and continues; (3) lets his enthusiasm diminish during the remainder of the demonstration; (4) allows his closing to become less assumptive—more of a suggestion than actually assuming the sale.

The prospect observes this, and he/she feels the salesperson is agreeing with the excuses. When this happens, the sale is lost.

Close and Keep Quiet

After a salesperson offers the choice questions in the assumptive close, he should keep quiet. The first one to break the silence loses. The salesperson should wait the prospect out until the prospect says something. Remember, the salesperson is waiting for an objection or an agreement to one of the choice questions.

It is tempting, if the prospect is slow in responding, to continue the demonstration. If the salesperson does this, the closing is wasted and the demonstrations damaged.

If a salesperson doesn't learn to close, or if he doesn't close, he will not get objections, but he won't get orders either.

Learn to Be a Good Listener

Salespeople all to often are taught to transmit, but not to receive.

The professional salesperson has learned the value of listening to his prospect to try to determine how the prospect really feels.

You will note the word "listens" throughout this book. Listening helps the prospect feel he is being talked with, not at. It creates the feeling that the salesperson is truly interested in the prospect, his concerns, his problems, and his welfare.

Some salespeople try to convey the idea that they are listening, when actually they are not. This is called negative listening. A person is negative listening when you try to present your ideas to which the other person may not agree, and as you explain your position you can see the other person thinking up how he is going to respond to you. He isn't hearing you at all. In essence, his response before he said a word is telling you he isn't interested in how you feel. This isn't the way to sell oneself to your prospects.

The negative-listening salesperson is so eager to answer the excuse that he may never let the prospect reveal his objections or concerns. The salesperson can't wait to jump on the excuse and eliminate it. The prospect gets to feeling that the salesperson is totally unsympathetic with the prospect's objection. This begins to become irritating. The prospect may interpret the salesperson's response as a lack of interest in him and his problems—only an interest in selling the product.

Not only does the professional salesperson listen; but he watches the prospect's body language, which may also convey to the salesperson how the prospect is responding or not responding to the ideas the salesperson is trying to sell. It is through listening to the prospect and watching the body language that the salesperson learns how the prospect is responding inside.

Don't Make the Prospect Feel He Is Your Adversary

Too many salespeople look upon a sales presentation as a contest between themselves and the prospect. This type of attitude puts the prospect on the defensive.

The salesperson must sell himself to his prospect at the very beginning of the sales presentation. Throughout the sales presentation the salesperson should convey the feeling that he is truly interested in the prospect's welfare.

If the prospect feels threatened he will cease to allow himself to enter into the presentation. That is why humor is so important. A salesperson must master the art of smiling while he talks.

When the prospect offers an objection, the salesperson should smile, agree, not take issue, and then offer an answer to the objection and proceed to create more need, use, and value.

It is easy to polarize oneself with a prospect by trying to hit on an objection head-on. Again the body language the salesperson assumes should have a very relaxed effect, hearing the objection, acknowledging it, and proceeding with more need, use, and value.

If the prospect finds that each time he offers an objection that the results are distasteful, he will withdraw from participation and he will close his mind. When this happens the sale is lost.

Chapter VIII

HANDLING
OBJECTIONS

PROFESSIONAL salespeople learn that there are many reasons why prospects object to buying. They know that the excuse the prospect gives is not necessarily true. They try to find the real reason for the objection. Unless they discover this reason, the objection cannot be overcome.

Emotional Blocks

In every presentation, emotions—both the salesperson's and the prospect's—are all important.

It is a mistake to assume that a logical presentation will motivate the prospect to buy. It is also a mistake to assume that the objections to buying are motivated by pure logic. However, the objections appear to be logical because the prospect wants the salesperson to believe him. That is why "buy later," "can't afford," "I want to think it over," are the most common objections. Who can best determine if I can or *cannot afford* to buy something? Who would question the wisdom of *thinking it over*? Who has the right to say I shouldn't *buy later*? Many times these excuses are a cover-up for the real reason. Frank Betteger in his book, *How I Raised Myself From a Failure to Success in Selling*, says that after he gets an objection, he says: "Mr. Prospect, besides that, what is the real reason for not buying today?" Often the prospect then tells him the real reason.

Pride

Pride is a powerful emotion. The following story of a personal experience will help the reader understand this emotion can supersede logic.

I was demonstrating a series of books for small children to a middle-aged father and mother. Their three-year-old daughter had been born after they almost had given up the hope of having children. Naturally, the girl was the most important thing in their lives.

After I demonstrated the books I closed with the subordinate choice technique. The father responded: "Mr. Bonnell, it looks like you have a good product and we are interested. Could you leave your card, or would you call me tomorrow, and I'll let you know our decision?" This was neither an objection or an agreement to buy. The father wanted to defer making a decision.

I smiled and replied: "Mr. Prospect, that would be fine. But when I explain these books to parents who are as dedicated to their children as you are to Mary, when parents show as much interest in the books as you have shown, then the parents say they want to think it over, it makes me feel that I have done a poor job of explaining the value of these books. If I had convinced you that these books would bring Mary the benefits you obviously want her to have, you would ask me how soon I could get them delivered, isn't that true?"

Now, I felt I was going to find the real reason for their hesitancy in buying.

The father said: "No. Forty-five minutes ago I never heard of these books. You come along, a complete stranger, and want me to make a snap decision. I never make snap decisions. I always sleep overnight before I make decisions."

This father probably read somewhere that Henry Ford, or another successful man, said: "Never make a hasty decision, sleep on it, then decide." This father always abided by the rule. He was proud of it, and he wasn't about to break the rule for me. This is pride; however, to him it was logic.

I felt that if I could get him to feel he had retained his pride, I could get the order now. My response went like this: "Mr. Prospect, I have a feeling that three years ago when the nurse placed this young lady in your arms, and you looked into those beautiful blue eyes for the first time, you decided right there what kind of a lady you wanted her to be when she was twenty. You decided whether you wanted Mary to grow up appreciating the best in children's literature or whether drugstore books would be all right for her. You decided that you wanted to answer her questions and keep alive her intellectual curiosity and confidence in you as her father. You decided that you wanted her to grow up appreciating art, music, and the cultural values. When you think about it, you decided three years ago to give Mary the benefits of these books. You just didn't know that there was anything like *Childcraft*, which would enable you to give her the values you decided you wanted her to have. This is no snap decision. You have been thinking about it for three years. Had you thought about it that way?''

The father answered: "No, I guess you are right." He now felt good about making the decision to buy. He retained his pride, and Mary got the books.

Think about some of the sales you have lost. Could it be that the prospect's motive for the excuse was pride?

Often the excuse "We pay cash" is motivated by pride. I know a manager who sold a father who gave this excuse. The father always paid cash, and he wasn't going to break his record. He was proud of that record, although he admitted his boys needed the *World Book Encyclopedia*.

The manager wisely agreed and said he wished he had a record like that. This caused the father, a farmer, to appreciate the salesperson because the salesperson appreciated and even envied his record. The salesperson suggested showing the order form to the farmer's wife, so that Mrs. Prospect could sign it and send in the payment. That way the farmer could keep his record intact and the children would have the books. The farmer agreed that this was a good solution.

It's difficult to know why people act the way they do. An experienced salesperson, however, learns through experience to look for the emotional block that must be removed before the prospect feels comfortable enough to buy.

Buying habits vary. Some people make decisions fast. Others feel insecure about buying on the first invitation. The latter feel better about a decision to buy if they have resisted, and the salesperson has created more need, use, and value. I presume they are avoiding the appearance of being easy to sell. This really is pride. The Chinese call it *saving face*.

Fear

Some people fear salesmen or saleswomen. They may have had bad experiences with high-pressure sellers. When a salesperson recognizes this, he or she should employ the soft-sell technique.

Usually the prospect who says he's not interested, "I'm not buying anything," is afraid he is going to buy. In these cases, the salesperson should create the feeling that he or she is almost indifferent about the sale. The salesperson might say: "Mr. Prospect, you may not even like my books, insurance policy, air conditioner, etc. Let's take a look at it. If you like it, fine. If you don't, that's fine too."

I tell prospects who even resist looking that I won't ask them to buy: "Let's look at it. Some day you may want to purchase books, insurance, an air conditioner, etc., and you will know then if you want to consider this product. It will take only a few minutes." Once the salesperson eliminates the threat of high-pressure, the prospect often becomes involved in the demonstration.

If the prospect appears interested in the benefits that the salesperson points out, but objects, this indicates the prospect's mental scale has not come into balance. The salesperson must create more need, use, and value.

The experienced salesperson wants to hear a prospect's excuse early in the interview. The amateur says: "Why would anyone want to hear an excuse?" The sale begins with the first excuse. The experienced salesperson knows that the objection will be either an *excuse* or a *reason*. He or she wants to treat the objection as an excuse until he or she is certain that it is an objection with which he or she must deal.

Step Number 1 — Ignore

The best response to the first objection is to ignore it. Smile and say, "I understand how you feel, but let me show you this feature of our product." Then proceed with more enthusiasm to explain the features and benefits.

Body Language

It is critical that the salesperson show no affects because of the objection. Your facial expression or tone of voice should not reveal any concern. To do so lends validity to the objection. A friendly, confident smile, agreement, and continuation of the presentation is the correct procedure.

No Pauses

To pause before responding to the objection may cause the prospect to feel that you are affected by the excuse. This, in turn, could cause him or her to feel that you agree with his objection.

It is said that a sale is made in every presentation — either the salesperson sells the prospect, or the prospect convinces the salesperson of the validity of his or her objections.

Step Number 2 — Treat Lightly

If the prospect offers an objection to the second closing, the salesperson should listen and determine if the objection has modified or weakened. If the second objection carries less conviction, it tells the salesperson that the prospect's mental scale is starting to balance in favor of buying.

Treat the objection lightly. You might smile and say: "I know how you feel, Mr. Prospect. Certainly we can't buy everything we want, but look at this as an investment which will pay off handsomely." Then proceed to show more features and benefits.

Employing this technique gives a prospect the feeling that you are sympathetic with his concern about the cost. But it also enables you to continue to create more need, use, and value.

At no time should you take direct issue with the prospect's excuse, or allow yourself to argue. It's tempting to win an argument, but when a salesperson wins the argument, he loses the sale.

Step Number 3 — Answer the Objection

If, after the third closing, the severity of the objection does not diminish, you must then answer the objection with the best logic you can muster. Once this is done, either review the features and benefits, or show additional features and benefits. Then close again. You might say: "Before I go, I do want to review the benefits you will receive by owning this product, etc."

Earlier I explained that two wills oppose each other in a presentation — the salesperson's will to persuade, and the prospect's will to resist. The will that weakens first strengthens the opposite will.

Sales resistance is perfectly normal, and the salesperson should expect it. After repeated objections, it is difficult for the salesperson to continue to close in an assumptive manner. However, if your body language, facial expressions, pauses, and lack of confidence indicate you have taken the objections seriously, the sale is lost.

A good rule-of-thumb is to ask for the order in a manner that conveys your confidence that the prospect will buy once he or she appreciates all the benefits of ownership.

If the salesperson becomes convinced that the prospect is not going to buy, he or she should graciously terminate the interview.

Humor

Two people laughing together are not far apart, as I have said before. Humor is an important ingredient in the art of persuasion. You can use humor to lessen the seriousness of an objection in the mind of the prospect. Remember, he wants you to agree with his objections.

A sales interview I once had demonstrates how humor can lessen the impact of an objection. I was demonstrating books to a young mother in Nashville, Tennessee. She was a graduate of Ward Belmont School, an exclusive girls' college. When I closed, she said that she had to discuss it with her husband, because it was his money and she didn't think she should spend his money without discussing it with him. This sounds like a logical, fair-minded reason with which she hoped that I would agree.

I smiled and said: "I have been trying to convince my wife of that same philosophy, but she keeps calling it our money. Can you imagine that? My wife has this crazy notion that by going through childbirth twice, taking the children to the doctor, doing the laundry, keeping the house clean, preparing meals, and shopping for groceries, she is making a contribution."

I gave her a sly smile to indicate I was not serious and continued, "I'd like to talk to your husband to learn how he talked you into the idea that it is his money. Maybe he could help me sell my wife on that idea. Now, Mrs. Prospect, I know you really don't believe it is his money."

The prospect laughed and said, "No, of course I don't."

I got off the subject, showed more need, use, and value, and got the order.

Be Natural

Closing should create a feeling that owning the product is normal and natural. A salesperson should never make the prospect feel that he or she is being asked to make a big decision. The salesperson wants the prospect to feel that buying the product is not an unusual thing to do. In fact, the salesperson should create the feeling that he or she would be surprised if the prospect didn't buy.

Reverse Sales Technique

Early in my selling career, when I needed and wanted orders badly, I missed a lot of sales because I tried too hard. The prospect became aware that I wanted the order, and this gave the wrong thrust to my demonstration. The emphasis was on what the order would do for me rather than on what owning the product would do for the prospect.

Some of the resistance of prospects is based on an assumption that the salesperson wants the order so badly he or she will do anything for it. If the salesperson's presentation indicates that this is true, the prospect, if so inclined, will dangle the salesperson on a string like a puppet.

People not in a position of authority can get considerable satisfaction from being in this position when they find themselves in front of a salesperson. It gives them a sense of control they do not enjoy in other contacts with people. In essence, they feel they own the salesperson. A professional salesperson never allows himself to be dominated or manipulated by a prospect. If this happens, the prospect loses respect for the salesperson.

If you create maximum need, use, and want for the product, and the prospect still resists buying, this is the time to employ reverse sales psychology. Assume the position of objectivity. Play the role of counselor, not salesperson.

You might say: "Mrs. Prospect, I have described the features and identified the benefits this widget will bring you. Yet, you obviously find it difficult to justify the investment. It is not my purpose to talk you into buying. All I want to do is to advise you of its features and benefits. You have to determine if it's worth the price. Maybe this just isn't for you."

If the prospect really is interested in the product, her/his resistance is due to the salesperson's overeagerness to get the order. Once you take an objective position, the prospect often moves closer to buying.

Caution—the reverse selling technique must be applied while the prospect's interest in buying is high.

This true story may help the reader understand this technique. During World War II, a young Air Force pilot dated a girl in the town where he was stationed. He proposed marriage several times, but the girlfriend remained uncommitted. She said that she would never leave the city where she lived. One day the officer received orders to transfer to another base, 1500 miles away. That evening he saw the girl. He mentioned early in the evening that he was being transferred, then said no more about it. He took his girlfriend to a movie, and on the way to her home she started crying. He asked her why she was crying. She said: "You're going to be transferred, and you haven't asked me to go with you." The officer reminded her that he had proposed marriage twice, and she said she would never leave the city. The result of this reverse technique was that the marriage date was set that night.

The reverse selling technique often enhances both the value of the product and the salesperson's image in the eyes of the prospect. More importantly, it enhances the salesperson's self-image. A professional salesperson never begs. Most people do not respect people they can dominate or intimidate. People are more apt to buy from successful people. A successful salesperson conveys a certain independence that an unsuccessful salesperson does not convey. When a salesperson needs a sale badly, he or she has a tendency to let it show. The prospect becomes aware of this and may feel the salesperson will do anything to get the order.

Another sales story will add an understanding of this psychology. I gave a presentation to a father who was interested in my books. I wrote up the order and he looked at it. He said that another salesperson recently had demonstrated a different set of books and had agreed to throw in a book rack free with the purchase. He asked me if I would give him a book rack if he bought. I replied: "No, I won't give you a book rack. Anytime someone wants to give you something to buy their product, there must be something wrong with the product. We give nothing free. We give the best product for the money.''

The prospect said: ''Yeah, I figure you're right.'' he signed the order.

There is no cause for a salesperson to lose dignity. I never thank a prospect for his/her time. But, I always terminate an interview tactfully, leaving the door open for another contact. It is my belief that the salesperson should terminate the sales presentation, not the prospect.

If convinced that I am not going to get the sale, I would rather terminate the interview by looking at my watch and saying, ''I have another appointment, so I must go.'' Having a sales demonstration terminated by a prospect's refusal to buy doesn't do my self-image any good.

Remember, maintain your dignity. You aren't your prospect's whipping boy or servant.

Chapter IX

EMOTIONS
IN THE
SALES INTERVIEW

As DISCUSSED in Chapter VIII, people are motivated more by their emotions than by logic. Let us examine further some of the emotions experienced by both the salesperson and the prospect.

Salesperson's Fears

A salesperson can experience many fears. If you are starting as a seller you may be afraid to contact your first customer. The beginning salesperson fears he or she will be rejected by the prospect.

Each of us has weaknesses that cause us to feel vulnerable. If a prospect refuses to see the salesperson, this can damage the ego. The salesperson has a message and no one wants to listen. He or she probably will be rejected more times than accepted. The greater the need for acceptance, the greater the damaging impact on the ego when a prospect refuses to see a salesperson.

Even if your approach to the customer is highly professional, your fear of rejection could cause you to appear less confident and assured. If a customer recognizes this, he or she may try to dominate you. Often the prospect feels no empathy for a salesperson and wants to manipulate him or her. For this reason, a company should send an experienced salesperson or manager with the new salesperson on his or her first call. This procedure helps lessen, modify, and put into proper perspective the rejection every salesperson must learn to live with.

Here is an example: When I took a new representative into the field he or she usually was apprehensive. If a housewife came to the door and said in a not-too-friendly way, "What do you want?" the representative found this a terrifying experience. Walking away from the home, I explained that the housewife probably was a nice person. I said that she might have been up all night with a sick child, or maybe had had an argument with her husband. I pointed out that we were tactful and polite, and did nothing to cause her to be rude. Therefore, I said, the housewife had a problem, we didn't. I turned this experience into a positive one by telling the new representative that I like selling because I can choose the people I deal with. Therefore, let us go to another home where the housewife doesn't have a problem. Unless a new salesperson is overly concerned about rejection, he or she will soon place all undesirable responses to his or her approaches in this perspective.

As a new salesperson experiences success, he or she gains self-confidence. This causes him to act and talk in an assured manner, and prospects respond to the salesperson's words, manner, and body language the way he or she expects them to respond. Although butterflies fly in formation in his stomach, he learns to hide fears, and gradually these fears diminish as more acceptance than rejection is experienced.

If you are totally sold on your mission, you eventually feel sorry for the prospect who refuses to see you. You no longer consider a prospect's refusal as a personal rejection.

Prospect's Fears

The prospect has fears, too. He or she has allowed a person into the home or office. That person is selling something and the prospect doesn't want to buy anything. At least he or she doesn't want to be sold anything.

This presents a problem to the salesperson because, unless the prospect's fears are removed, the prospect will open his or her mind to the ideas the salesperson wants to get across. The experienced salesperson knows this, so he spends the first few minutes of the interview developing rapport with the prospect.

Forget Selling the Product — SELL YOURSELF

To sell himself, a professional salesperson will try to

find an area of common interest with the prospect. If the size of the sales plus repeat business is important, some pre-calling research to learn as much about the prospect as possible regarding hobbies, interests, company, family, etc., may be worthwhile. If the item will not involve repeat business or pre-calling research, a salesperson should find areas of common interests early in the interview.

Most of the selling I did for forty years involved calling on homes to sell *The World Book Encyclopedia*. Usually, I had no information on the prospect. In all instances they had children. Once in a home I tried to spot evidence of a hobby, such as cameras, painting, sewing, etc. Usually, the living room is the showcase of a family's taste and interest. Usually, I would spot pictures of the children. The picture on the mantel, or piano, told me that I could gain acceptance and rapport by asking questions such as: "Are these Johnny's and Mary's pictures?" "How old were they when these pictures were taken?" "They certainly are bright-looking children." "How old is Johnny now?" "What grade is he in?"

The mother, to whom I hope to sell my products, was beginning to warm up to me. When asking these questions, I did so in a manner that indicates true interest in the children. Gradually, apprehension and concern about my mission lessened as we engaged in a friendly, sometimes humorous, conversation about her children.

If a technique becomes obvious, it causes resentment, so the prospect must feel you are genuinely interested. When a salesperson calls on me and starts telling me what a terrific-looking suit I have on, and it is obvious that he has been trained to do so, I turn him out rapidly. Usually, people do not like to be patronized.

Once a prospect's fears and apprehension are removed, you can move into the formal part of your sales presentation.

How To Identify Prospect Fear

Usually a prospect's body language indicates his or her fears. If he or she smiles little, sits rigid, and speaks only when necessary, he or she is probably apprehensive.

If the prospect doesn't warm up, you can meet the problem directly by asking: "Mr./Mrs. Brown, are you apprehensive about my calling on you?"

Usually, this causes him to reveal his fears. Expressing concern over his feelings will do much to put him at ease.

Cause of Prospect's Fears

Many people fear they will be sold something. This often is due to the fact they were sold something once and "buyer's remorse" set in after the sale. Also, some people have been treated badly by salespeople using high-pressure methods. Because of this, they distrust themselves in a selling situation and they distrust salespeople. They are afraid to interact with the salesperson. Unless the salesperson can eliminate this fear and gain the confidence of the prospect, the salesperson is probably wasting time.

"No-Nonsense" Prospect

Every salesperson who has made lots of sales contacts encounters the "no-nonsense — tell me what it costs" prospect. Usually, this kind of response early in the interview indicates that the prospect is fearful he or she will be sold something. He or she is putting up defenses at the beginning. This type of prospect terrifies the inexperienced seller. But, the experienced salesperson knows this type often is the easiest to sell. The prospect knows this, too, that's why the defensive, no-nonsense reaction. Knowing the prospect's fears of buying, the experienced salesperson tries to eliminate any feeling that he or she is trying to sell the prospect. The salesperson might say: "Mr. Prospect, I can appreciate your concern for what this product costs, because we can't afford everything. But, why don't we take a look at it. You may find out you don't even want it."

Nonresponsive Prospect

Every experienced salesperson also encounters the prospect who does not respond when the salesperson points out the benefits of his or her product. Giving a demonstration to this type of prospect can be exasperating — the prospect doesn't agree or disagree, doesn't seem interested or not interested. The prospect does not give you any clue about the balance of his or her mental scale. Usually, the more effort you make to elicit a response, the more exasperated you become. In my experience, continuing the interview without any clue about the prospect's interest increases the exasperation. Stop the interview, smile, and say: "Mr. Prospect, we know all people are not interested in this product, however, there is no way of knowing who is interested until all the features and benefits have been explained to the people we call on. I get the feeling you are not too interested; if you are not, you would be doing me a favor by telling me so. Do you see any benefits in this product to you?" Usually the prospect's response tells the salesperson if he or she is wasting time.

Reason for Lack of Response

A prospect does not respond to the salesperson's efforts for three reasons:

1. He or she is an unresponsive type of person. This type may be interested but shows no response.
2. The prospect is fearful that he or she will be sold and doesn't want the salesperson to know it.
3. The prospect is not interested and merely tolerates the salesperson.

The procedure mentioned above should tell you which reason applies to a prospect.

Although the prospect owes the salesperson nothing, there is no reason why a salesperson should waste valuable time. The salesperson has a right to know how the prospect feels. If the prospect has listened to enough of the presentation to know he or she is not interested, no benefit accrues to either the salesperson or the prospect by continuing the interview.

Chapter X

TIME

THREE THINGS determine how many sales a seller consummates in any given period of time:

1. Number of sales presentations.
2. Techniques employed by the salesperson.
3. Third-party influence that the salesperson can use to help the prospect buy.

Time is a precious commodity to a salesperson. To a salaried person working in an office, time is not as critical. Someone once said that if a salesperson isn't in front of a prospect, the salesperson is unemployed.

The number of demonstrations in any period of time depends on the salesperson's method of working. Any system that reduces the number of presentations is the wrong system.

A salesperson's day should be well planned. Most sellers learn when their most productive selling time is. Some sell best in the evening; for others morning is the most productive time. A salesperson should be very careful how he invests this time, called "High Productive Time."

Once a salesperson calculates the dollar value of his time, he can see what is costs to waste or misuse it.

Third-Party Influence

Sales techniques and third-party influence both will determine how many sales presentations result in sales. Sales techniques have been suggested. Now, I want to comment on third-party influence.

At the point of decision, if you can show letters from owners, or from authorities endorsing the product, it reassures the prospect that buying the product is the thing to do. Most people are followers, so a good salesperson provides statements of endorsement or approval of the product to favorably influence the prospect.

Assume I have given a sales presentation of *World Book* to a parent. The parent decided to buy and is ready to sign the order. Suppose I said, "Mrs. Prospect, I think that you should know that you are the first parent in this community to buy *World Book*." The prospect is going to put down the pen and not sign the order. She doesn't want to be first. She doesn't mind being fiftieth, but not first.

An owner's list is a valuable item for a salesperson to carry and show the prospect. Seeing the names of people who have bought the product reassures the prospect that buying is the right thing to do.

Once I observed one of our managers in Scotland make a sales presentation. After we left the prospect's home, the manager prepared his sales kit for the next interview. He was going to tear out the order we had just written. I suggested he leave it in his order book, so the next prospect could see that someone else bought that evening in the same neighborhood.

Chapter XI

MORALE

ONE OF THE main reasons people enter sales and fail is not a lack of potential for selling, but because they cannot cope with the problems a seller must face.

Failure Experiences

The salesperson must learn to live with the idea that he will fail to sell more often than he will succeed. In most jobs people do not experience more failures than successes. People working in an office usually do not have to get up in the morning to face another day when they felt they failed the previous day. The office worker's income does not fluctuate like that of the commission salesperson.

Many sellers interpret getting an order as success and not getting an order as failure. The experienced, successful salesperson learns that not getting an order is only a part of a process by which he gives a certain number of presentations, applying all his sales skills and knowledge. The salesperson knows that "X" number of demonstrations will result in "X" number of sales.

The salesperson must have the same attitude as a researcher. The latter knows that he must fail more often than he succeeds. What if a person said, "I want to go into research, but I want to discover what I am searching for on the first attempt."

Law of Averages

Every salesperson, baseball batter, football quarterback—in fact, nearly every professional—operates on the law of averages. I have assigned this equation to the seller's law of averages:

$$100 \text{ SP} + \text{CMA} + \text{CT} = \text{CNO}$$

It means: 100 *sales presentations*, given with a *constant mental attitude* plus a *constant technique* equals a *constant number of orders*.

The big variable in that equation is mental attitude. Technique does not change much from day to day, but mental attitude can vary greatly. Experiences that cause it to fluctuate are the presentations that fail to produce an order, and presentations that succeed. This fluctuation creates the unavoidable pattern that is a problem. For instance, in the company I work with we know that the national average is one sale from five presentations.

If we could assure each salesperson that after five presentations he or she would be guaranteed an order, there would be no problem. If we could guarantee this kind of results, we could hire people easily. The commission on one order for five demonstrations enables the salesperson to have a good income. Knowing he was going to obtain this kind of income would relieve the salesperson of the need to develop perseverance, self-discipline, self-motivation, and all the qualities salespeople must develop. In fact, the position could become quite routine. Unfortunately, this cannot be done. Unless the salesperson develops total faith that the law of averages will work in the long run, he will always be insecure in selling.

Analyzing Results

Salespeople, by nature, do not like to write reports and keep records. They detest statistics. However, when playing golf or tennis, salespeople will keep a score card. When asked why he or she does this, the seller will say, "I want to know how I'm doing."

It seems incredible that these same people will not analyze their selling results so that they can see how they are doing. I've seen salespeople become discouraged because they thought they were not doing well, when, in fact, they were doing fine. Let me give you an example: I had a salesperson who had sold successfully for several years. She kept records of the hours she worked, the presentations she made, and the ratio of sales per demonstration. Unfortunately, she didn't study and analyze these performance records.

One day she came into my office looking discouraged. She thought something was wrong with her presentation and asked me to go with her on a call. I agreed to do this, but I asked her to bring her records into the office first. I knew that her technique could not have changed dramatically. She thought something was wrong because the previous two weeks she sold only three orders per week. Normally, she obtained five or six orders per week.

When she brought in her records, I asked her to total how many full weeks in the past year that she had worked. Then I asked her to calculate the orders she had sold, divide the number of weeks into the total orders, and see what she averaged each week. She discovered that she averaged five orders per week. I asked her to add up the weeks in which she had sold seven orders and the weeks in which she had sold three orders. The answers came out about the same. This proved to her that she had about as many weeks when she sold two orders above average as weeks when she had sold two below average.

As I examined here weekly performance, I found periods of three weeks in succession when she sold six, seven, and eight orders. I reminded her that she didn't come into my office when this happened, wanting to return part of her earnings because she felt she was overpaid. She accepted the unusually good weeks, but when two substandard weeks occurred back-to-back, she became discouraged. She was doing fine, but didn't know it. It isn't always what really happens that affects a salesperson's morale, it's what she thinks has happened. No salesperson should allow this to happen.

Every seller should keep a highly visible record of his or her results. You can design your own. In this one (see page 106), each square represents a sales demonstration. When a sale is made, that square should be colored red. When you make a presentation and don't get the sale, color that square blue.

The ratio of sales to demonstrations fluctuates and patterns can be erratic even though your technique does not change. Some weeks everything turns to gold — you sell on nearly every demonstration. The next week your performance may be well below average. It is these weeks that can cause trouble. However, if you keep a chart on a monthly basis, you will note that, although the patterns can vary dramatically, the law of averages remains relatively constant. Once you develop faith in the law of averages, your morale won't fluctuate from day to day, or week to week, like a roller coaster.

Confidence in the law of averages influences the salesperson to go after good, qualified sales presentations, not orders. If the seller gets the presentations that he should get in a week, the seller knows the orders will come.

The best thing you can have is a chart showing ten to twelve demonstrations in a row with no sales, yet the ratio of sales to presentations remains good for the month. This chart forces you to realize that unusual patterns happen again and again. Why it happens, I don't know. Why a baseball player who hits 300, suddenly goes to bat ten times without a hit, cannot be explained either. But it happens. Looking at the chart, knowing it happened before — but that the law of averages held over the year or month — lessens the negative effect such experiences have on morale.

Sales Progress Chart

Here's an easy tool to chart your selling progress.
Each square represents one complete demonstration.
Just color the appropriate square blue when you've
achieved a sale and red if a sale was not made.

| 1 | 2 | 3 | 4 | 5 | 6 | 7 | 8 | 9 | 10 |
| □ | □ | □ | □ | □ | □ | □ | □ | □ | □ |

| 11 | 12 | 13 | 14 | 15 | 16 | 17 | 18 | 19 | 20 |
| □ | □ | □ | □ | □ | □ | □ | □ | □ | □ |

| 21 | 22 | 23 | 24 | 25 | 26 | 27 | 28 | 29 | 30 |
| □ | □ | □ | □ | □ | □ | □ | □ | □ | □ |

| 31 | 32 | 33 | 34 | 35 | 36 | 37 | 38 | 39 | 40 |
| □ | □ | □ | □ | □ | □ | □ | □ | □ | □ |

| 41 | 42 | 43 | 44 | 45 | 46 | 47 | 48 | 49 | 50 |
| □ | □ | □ | □ | □ | □ | □ | □ | □ | □ |

| 51 | 52 | 53 | 54 | 55 | 56 | 57 | 58 | 59 | 60 |
| □ | □ | □ | □ | □ | □ | □ | □ | □ | □ |

| 61 | 62 | 63 | 64 | 65 | 66 | 67 | 68 | 69 | 70 |
| □ | □ | □ | □ | □ | □ | □ | □ | □ | □ |

| 71 | 72 | 73 | 74 | 75 | 76 | 77 | 78 | 79 | 80 |
| □ | □ | □ | □ | □ | □ | □ | □ | □ | □ |

Range of Goals

Minimum Acceptable	
Average Expected	
Maximum Probable	

DAILY PERFORMANCE RECORD

1	2	3	4	5
Date	*No. of Hours Worked	*No. of Demonstrations	No. of Sales	Commissions on Sales
				$
Totals				$

*Count Only Actual Hours in the Field and Complete Demonstrations

Sales Progress Chart

Name_____

Address_____

City_____

Branch_____

_____
(Month)

Financial Goal

Minimum Acceptable	Average Expected	Maximum Probable
$	$	$

RECAPITULATION AND EVALUATION OF PROGRESS

(Refer to your Daily Performance Record for accurate totals.)

1. Total hours worked (Column 2)_____

2. Number of demonstrations (Column 3)_____

3. Total sales (Column 4)_____

4. Average number of demonstrations per sale_____

5. Total commissions on sales (Column 5)_____

6. Earnings per demonstration $_____

7. Was goal achieved?   Yes ☐   No ☐

Morale Affects Techniques

If your morale is low, it affects your technique. You may say the words and go through the motions, but you lack enthusiasm and expectancy for the order. When a salesperson hits a slump, he or she tends to change the presentation. Baseball hitters in a slump often do the same thing. They change their stance or swing. Usually this prolongs the slump. A salesperson should continue employing the same techniques and procedures he knows will bring orders. If the seller does, the law of averages never fails.

Record Sales to Order Ratio

On the progress chart, a salesperson should note total hours worked for the month, sales, commissions, and orders. The salesperson should record the number of presentations required to get an order, the true measure of his effectiveness. The salesperson should compete with himself, trying to improve the sales-to-presentation ratio each month.

A smart seller wants to know how much each hour and each presentation is worth, whether or not a sale is made. Knowing this helps the seller appreciate that he is paid for every presentation given. This produces good morale and a more conscientious use of time.

You should be vitally interested in recording and analyzing your performance. You should know what's happening just as business owners keep records and accounts to determine the profitability of his business. Guessing is hazardous and costly.

Avoiding Erroneous Judgments

Here is another illustration to help you better appreciate the value of keeping a Sales Progress Chart.

Assume you are employed to sell an item with a commission of $70.00 per sale. Your sales presentation averages one to one and a half hours. On a good day, you give five sales presentations.

Like the average salesperson you make one sale out of every five presentations. The first month you give 100 presentations and get 20 sales. You have done as well as the average salesperson and should be pleased with your income.

On the first day you begin your second 100 presentations, you make three presentations by 1 P.M. and get three sales. Your mental attitude soars. You say to yourself, "This is a great business." You worked from 9 A.M. to 1 P.M. and made $210.00. Because your earnings are so dramatic, you can calculate that you earned $210.00 in four hours. More than $50.00 per hour. Normally, you take one to one and a half hours for lunch, but you say to yourself, if I earn $50.00 per hour, I can't afford a one-hour lunch. You grab a sandwich and go back to making calls. You give two presentations in the afternoon and get no sales. The next day, you give five presentations and get no sales. Now you tell yourself that this is an insecure business. It's boom or bust — feast or famine.

You no longer assume the sale because you don't expect anyone to buy. About the only way you can get an order is for someone to take the product away from you. You think something is wrong. But nothing is wrong. You think you earned $210.00 on three presentations, but according to the law of averages, you have to give 12 more presentatives without sales to earn $210.00.

When a person thinks they aren't doing well, even though they are, they are discouraged. Discouragement affects their motivation and sales technique. If salespeople kept a Sales Progress Chart, they would know what's going on. They would not be less affected negatively by the extreme patterns that all salespeople experience. A person is as he thinketh.

Why it Pays to Know What's Going on

Assume that you increase your sales-to-presentation ratio by 0.5 percent from the first 100 to the second 100 presentations. That means five more sales at $70.00 each, or a $350.00 increase. If you don't keep score, you may not be aware of such improvements in selling average. This would rob you of an excellent motivator and morale builder — the awareness that you made progress. When a person makes progress and doesn't realize it, he is just as discouraged as if they weren't making progress.

I recommend that every salesperson keep score. Set a goal each month to increase the number of presentations, and to reduce the number of presentations needed to get an order.

Chapter XII

POSITIVES FROM NEGATIVES

HISTORY BOOKS are full of stories about people who rise above disaster and handicaps that once seemed to blot out all hope for achievement. One is the story of Glenn Cunningham who was burned in a schoolhouse fire. Doctors predicted that he wouldn't walk, yet he became one of the greatest mile runners. A friend of mine, Dave Yoho, was born with a mouth defect. He took speech therapy and learned more about elocution than most speakers ever know. His weakness became his strength.

Every person experiences events that appear disastrous. It's how a person reacts to these events that is important. Much of the philosophy I live by originated with events that appeared harmful to my career. But because I stayed with my profession, I gleaned the positives that accrued from these events. Often events that appear ruinous force us to overcome problems we think we could never handle. I learned not to pass judgment on such events until I can assess the positives I might glean from them.

Occasionally, I attempt to recruit people who have never sold. These people wanted to enter sales, but didn't have the courage to leave a salaried position. When they lost the position, they joined my company and were successful.

I began my selling career in 1938, at the close of the Big Depression. There were times when I wanted to quit, but there were no jobs available. If someone had offered me a job for $5,000 a year, I might have taken it. Because I had no choice, I stayed with selling. Now, of course, I'm grateful. When you are discouraged you don't think rationally. At such times, a salesperson often makes a decision based on emotion that may be regretted later. Someone has said, if you are going to quit salesmanship, do it after you have a successful week. Go out a winner. Of course, winners don't quit.

Mental Attitude

I know of no other profession where mental attitude plays such as important role. Enthusiasm is vital to every sales presentation. A salesperson can be sold on his or her product, but if he or she isn't selling much it's hard to be enthusiastic. Most sales positions take the very best a person has to become successful. Most jobs do not constantly require a person's best efforts. For the average position you don't need to be in a positive frame of mind each morning. You don't have to be enthusiastic enough to influence someone.

Structuring

Most jobs are much more highly structured than sales work. A person in an office doesn't have to decide each day when and where he or she should work. In many sales positions, the salesperson has these choices to make every working day.

An office worker rarely goes home at night feeling that he or she has failed or wasted the entire day. A salesperson often goes home with these feelings.

The office worker knows he or she will be rewarded for his or her efforts. The salesperson, unless sold on the law of averages, isn't convinced he or she is going to be rewarded for the week's work.

Solution

The salesperson must plan and structure his or her week. An unplanned day invites laziness, inefficiency, and decreased motivation. A salesperson should prepare mentally for each day. Reading inspirational books or listening to tapes for 15 minutes before he or she starts the day will help.

Law of Averages

The salesperson must believe that everyday's work will be rewarded.

Chapter XIII

WHICH
WILL IT BE

No one forces us to choose between achievement and mediocrity, or success or failure. We are the architects of our futures. It is by our own design that we become what we are.

Everyone is offered choices. Some of them present challenges and problems, and demand that we grow inside. Others demand little and present few fears or risks. They reward us with comfort and tranquility, but rob us of opportunity to create, influence others, serve importantly, and enhance our self-image.

Let's look at some of these choices.

Positive or Negative Thoughts

You have free choice of the thoughts that you keep in your mind. Positive thoughts produce positive results. Negative thoughts produce negative results. You can choose to feed your mind with positive thoughts that create success. Conversely, you can nurture your mind with negative thoughts that defeat you.

Advice

You may choose to seek and follow the advice of successful people or you can seek and follow the advice of average people. If you want to make $50,000 a year, you shouldn't ask the person making $10,000 how to do it.

Average thinkers surround us. It's easy to listen to average people because there are so many of them. Their advice will give you comfort because it involves no risks, no challenges, and no attempts to achieve. The siren songs of average people offer a false sense of security that justifies not trying.

Job — or — Opportunity

Every person can choose between a job and an opportunity.

A job offers regular hours, a guaranteed salary and, often, routine, structured activities. These activities do not require self-discipline or a positive mental attitude. They present few challenges and few disappointments or discouragements. The average job offers limited control over the future, little independence, and restricted potential income.

An opportunity usually involves risks, long hours, challenges, and the possibility of occasional failure. It also offers the opportunity for creativity and ingenuity. It includes greater potential for controlling advancement and, for successful people, more security and independence.

Image—Choices

You can choose to develop a good image of yourself through achievement, or you can allow others to direct your destiny by seeking and being concerned about their approval. If you have your own approval, you don't need the approval of others. As Emerson said: "What you are speaks so loudly, I can't hear what you are saying."

People without money often surround themselves with trappings that they think will impress those whose approval they seek, because they don't have their own approval. This is why many college graduates do not apply for sales positions. They fear their relatives and friends would not approve.

Fears

We all have things that we fear — things we have not yet mastered. We can face these fears and conquer them, or we can accommodate them and permit them to dominate us all of our lives.

Courage is not the absence of fear, it is the conquest of it. Emerson wrote: "If we do the things we fear, the death of fear is certain."

Realism or Fantasy

You can choose to see life as it is, understanding that

the rules of success are tough. Or you can live in a world of fantasy, believing you can make it big without adhering to the rules of success. When you make yourself believe you are living by the rules, but you aren't, you deceive yourself. When you deceive yourself, you're the loser.

You can choose *fantasy* or *reality*.

Commitment or Noncommitment

A commitment to a goal is frought with fears. It is less demanding to remain uncommitted. However, the price of noncommitment is mediocrity.

It requires courage, self-discipline, and positive qualities to commit oneself to a goal. To be uncommitted is safer, comfortable, and tranquil. You choose the course you take and the rewards you get.

Long-Range or Short-Range Thinking

Every person can choose to make decisions for immediate gain, or choose to sacrifice immediate gain for long-range growth.

The average person chooses immediate gain. He or she doesn't have faith in things unseen. Taking one step backwards to be able to take three steps forward in the future is not conceivable to them. They choose the immediate gain to reap the quick reward.

The most successful people are more concerned with

where decisions will take them three years, five years, or more from now. They, too, reap rewards.

Self-Discipline or No Discipline

You can learn to discipline yorself, or you can permit outside influences to charter your course. Both have their own rewards. Keep in mind that each one of us is the architect of his or her own future. The designs we use are the choices we make.

To Pay the Price of Success or the Price of Mediocrity

We pay a price for success. But mediocrity also has a price: lack of good self-image, lack of respect, lack of income. A mediocre person can't pay cash for his or her car, can't afford to travel to places he or she would like to go, can only window-shop in exclusive stores. Both the mediocre person and the family pay the price for mediocrity.

It's up to each of us to pay the price for success and enjoy the fruits of high achievement, or pay the price of mediocrity.

REMEMBER, when you are making a choice, average thinkers who are ready with advice will never encourage you to make the choices that create success.

Chapter XIV

YOU CAN
BE BETTER
THAN YOU ARE

MOST PEOPLE want to achieve, but some have given up on themselves. This book is written for those who still have the will to succeed.

My forty years of working with people trying to be achievers convinces me that, if you look in a mirror, you see your greatest problem. Said another way, you don't have to tell people what to do to become better, because they already know. For instance, a person who is overweight doesn't need to be told he should lose weight. He knows that, but he isn't doing it.

We all have fears, complexes, inhibitions, and bad habits that limit our potential. Some of these problems were unintentionally implanted by our parents. These mental hangups may not be incapacitating, but they keep us from realizing our full potential.

I think of achievers as being on the *mountain* and nonachievers as being in the *valley*. There are far more people in the valley than on the mountain. In my judgment,

several reasons account for this. Most people are pro-
grammed to be average by parents, friends, and associates.
We are surrounded by average thinkers who believe in immediate gain at the expense of long-range loss.

Think

People live in the valley rather than on the mountain
because they think like valley people. They listen to the
advice of valley people.

One reason why valley people place so much credence
in average advice is that there is so much of it. They say
everybody can't be wrong. However, I learned a long time
ago that if I followed the advice of average people, I would
achieve no more than they do.

The company I work for recruits teachers to sell our
products in summer months. If a teacher does well, we try
to persuade him or her to join the company on a full-time
basis. Usually we have a wine-and-dine session with the
teacher and his or her spouse. After that interview the
teacher goes back to school, and fellow teachers ask what
the *World Book* manager offered. When the teacher tells
them, the fellow teachers advise him or her not to leave
teaching. As I mentioned before, if you want to make
$50,000 per year, don't ask a person making $10,000 a
year how to do it.

Valley people show no faith in things unseen. If they
can't wear it, ride it, eat it, or be entertained by it, they
place no value on it. Valley people make decisions on the

basis of immediate gain. They find it difficult to sustain interest in activities that will, down the road, bring benefits.

Security

Valley people are typically concerned about security.

But, where does one get security? Security comes from within. You cannot guarantee me security; I'm the only one who can guarantee me security. *Security comes with mastering a skill that is in great demand.*

We are rearing a generation of young people today who want their security guaranteed from cradle to grave by the federal government, or they want to join something and vote for the benefits, or get them in some other means besides working. That's why the socialistic and communistic philosophy attracts so many people today.

Personally, I will buy that philosophy when the good Lord creates us with the same drives, wants, ambitions, and when everyone makes the same contribution. Since each of us is the architect of his or her future, we cannot place the responsibility into someone else's hands.

I managed my company's Canadian operation for three years. One day, in downtown Vancouver, I caught a taxi to my motel room in the suburbs. A young fellow drove the cab. I asked him if he drove a taxi full-time. He said no, it was part-time work. He told me he was a student at the University of British Columbia. I asked him if he had a job for the coming summer. He replied that he had a good job waiting tables. I told him I employed people for the summer to sell the *World Book Encyclopedia*. Here was his answer — the answer of a man twenty-three years old who prepared himself for life's work with this concept of security: "That's a commission job, isn't it?" he asked.

"Yes, the more you sell, the more you get paid — the less you sell, the less you get paid," I answered.

"I want no part of working on a commission. I would rather work for less money and know I'm going to get a paycheck each week, than to take on anything as chancey as commission selling."

This young man's concept of security consisted of finding work where there is no chance to fail, no challenges, no risk, but a paycheck each week. If a person has that concept of security, I can tell him how to get it easier than working — rob a bank and get caught. He will get three meals a day and a place to sleep.

Without risk, there is little opportunity. The sure things don't pay off much.

James Byrnes said: "Too many people are thinking of security instead of opportunity. They seem more afraid of life than death."

Abraham Lincoln said: "You cannot strengthen the weak by weakening the strong. . . . You cannot help the wage earner by pulling down the wage payer. . . . You cannot further the brotherhood of men by encouraging class hatred. . . . You cannot help the poor by discouraging the rich. . . . You cannot build character and courage by taking away a man's initiative and independence."

John Stuart Mill said: "A state which dwarfs its men, in order that they may be more docile instruments in its hands even for beneficial purposes — will find that with small men no great things can really be accomplished.''

The Struggle

Valley people do not like to struggle. They love the comfort of not facing challenges and problems.

Achievement is related to struggle. Sir Edmund Hillary was knighted for climbing Mt. Everest (29,028 feet), not for climbing Mt. McKinley (20,320 feet).

In my early selling years, I used to get discouraged. The company didn't have sales meetings in those days, and I would not see another person who was doing what I was doing for months at a time. Naturally, I had negative experiences and failures. I knew it was important to feed my mind with positive thoughts and inspiration from other people, so I started reading biographies and autobiographies of successful people. I found a common experience in all of these books. Every one of these great people revealed that a struggle was involved in their success. I was having a terrific struggle, so I figured I was on the right track.

I accepted that I would never achieve things without a struggle. Valley people avoid struggle, which is one of the main reasons they stay in the valley.

Fear of Failure

Art Mortell, in his book, *The Anatomy of a Successful*

Salesman, notes that much of society resists an attempt at high achievement for fear of failure.

Failure is a great teacher — it's the way we learn most of the important lessons of life. Of course, if a person doesn't try, he won't fail, but he won't achieve much either.

Courage is not the absence of fear — it's the conquest of fear. Emerson said, "Do the things you fear and the death of fear is certain."

We are not born with courage; we develop it by facing our fears. Succumbing to these fears strengthens their hold on us. Have you ever been to a big dinner where they honored the man-of-the-year by saying: "We honor Henry tonight; he made it to the top with no guts"?

Discouragement is perfectly normal when you try to climb a mountain.

When a person in our business is beginning his career, it also is perfectly normal to get discouraged. It is easy, too, for new sales managers to feel they are not suited for this business. They never see their manager discouraged. They never see people from the home office discouraged. But they didn't see us when we started. I could tell you stories of discouragement that would ruin your whole day. What everyone must learn from this is that things will not always be that way.

Lack of Commitment

Valley people will not commit themselves to achieve — to get out of the valley. It takes courage to burn bridges so that there is no retreat or surrender.

Every war spawns stories of great heroism by men never thought of as heroes. These men found themselves in positions where there was only one way to survive — fight their way out. They found inner resources they never knew they had. To deliberately choose to place oneself in such a position takes much courage — courage valley people don't possess.

Unless a person "burns his bridges" and eliminates thoughts like "What will I do if I fail," he never discovers the extent of those resources. Several years ago, I managed one of my company's sales zones. A young teacher who had sold for us during several summers expressed interest in joining the company full-time. He did fairly well, but had one problem each morning — getting out his own door to make sales calls.

One day I received a call from his branch manager. He thought that this new recruit wanted to go back to teaching. He contemplated placing the young man on a $200 per week guarantee, and asked me what I thought of the idea. I didn't think much of it, and asked what the guarantee would do for the new man. The branch manager said he wanted to save him for the business. I commented that his problem involved lack of self-discipline. To pay him $200 a week because he could not discipline himself would break one of the basic rules for success. If this young man could not learn to manage himself, he didn't have a future with our company.

The branch manager told me that the young man was in his office and asked me to talk with him. Our long-distance phone interview went like this:

> Howard: "Dick [not his real name], what's this I hear about you going back to teaching?"
>
> Dick: "Well, I guess I made a mistake coming into this business."
>
> Howard: "Dick, let me tell you something. You are not contemplating returning to your old job because you prefer teaching; you're running away from yourself."
>
> Dick: "What do you mean?"
>
> Howard: "Your big problem is getting out your own door, isn't that right?"
>
> Dick: "I didn't realize there was so much self-discipline involved in this work"
>
> Howard: "Now wait a minute, Dick, when we interviewed you for this work you represented yourself as being ambitious. You wanted to serve importantly, you wanted to make big money and move up the promotional ladder. Surely you are mature enough to realize that the higher you go in rank, the more self-discipline it takes. You have children, don't you, Dick?"
>
> Dick: "Yes, I do."
>
> Howard: "Aren't you going to teach them self-discipline?"
>
> Dick: "Of course."
>
> Howard: "They will grow up and find out their father doesn't have self-discipline. Dick, you can't live one way and preach another to your children. If you sign up to teach and the school board says you have to be in the classroom at 8:00 A.M. each morning, you will be there. Isn't that right?"
>
> Dick: "Yes."
>
> Howard: "You are telling me that you feel a higher sense of responsibility toward a school board than you

do toward yourself and your family. Dick, I have observed you give sales demonstrations and you are good. You have a lot of talent, but you entertain the idea of running away from that talent and resigning yourself to a life of mediocrity. I thought there was more to you than that."

[I want to make it clear that I respect dedicated teachers. Keep in mind that Dick joined our company seeking benefits he could not get as a teacher. He knew he could return to teaching and avoid the self-discipline and perseverance his sales management position demanded if he wanted to be successful.]

Howard: "Every person trying to climb the ladder of success has conferences with himself along the way. Someone once said that the nice thing about these conferences is that you can have them any time, because you're available.

"Dick, let me tell you about a conference I had with myself early in my career. It went like this: Howard, do you want to be successful? Yes, I do, I answered. Do you want to serve importantly, make a lot of money, and be looked up to with respect? I replied that those were my goals. Then I said to myself: Do you know any college classmates who get those benefits and go to work later than 9:00 A.M. each day?

"I had to admit that my college friends who were moving up with other companies came to work at 8:00 A.M. I then said to myself: If you are going to get those benefits, then perhaps you should be at the first call at 9:00 A.M. — not 9:01, or 9:05, but 9:00 A.M.

"I agreed that I couldn't afford the luxury of being at home after 8:30 A.M. Also, I agreed that if I kept a schedule of being at the first call at 9:00 A.M. for three months, I wouldn't have to work at that problem any more — it would become habitual.

"Dick, I made that commitment to myself and in three months I had that 'monkey' off my back. I then started on other monkeys that dominated or hurt me, and twenty years ago I buried most of them. Now, Dick, if you haven't got the guts to do that, then you should get a job where you have to show up each morning or you will get fired."

A month later, Dick attended an achievement conference and got caught up in the dynamics of that meeting. When he returned home, he sent me the following letter: "Dear Howard: I have not made the progress I should, but I know whose fault this is. That is over. I am on my way. Keep this letter on file. If I ever get down again, send it to me as a reminder."

I learned that after returning from the conference, he went to his school board and asked them to take his name off the list as a prospective teacher. Before this, Dick had not been totally committed to his new career. He didn't have the courage to cut the umbilical cord with the school system. His idea was to stick one foot in our business and see how it went. If it got too tough, he wanted a place to which he could retreat. After Dick burnt his bridges, he had to draw on all his resources, skills, and talents. He now holds the top field management position in our company.

When Dick was promoted to branch manager, he wrote me the following letter. "Dear Howard: As you can well imagine, this past weekend was a mountain-top experience. What really topped it off was the letter Bill gave me to open from you. What does one say in words about the influence you have had over my business career? I don't believe it can be expressed. Putting it in a nutshell: deep gratitude and excitement, gratitude for your kick in the seat of my pants, and excitement at being able to gain personally from our continued association.''

Many people have the same problem. Lack of achievement is not always due to lack of talent. When a person is only partially committed, he is not bringing all his talents and energy to play.

People who approach a difficult goal with "I'll try," or "I'll do my best," give themselves an "out." When a person works at an occupation which constantly presents challenges, and is totally committed to meeting those challenges, he will draw upon inner resources that ordinarily are never tapped.

Leterman in his book, *Personal Power Through Creative Selling,* says: "Confidence is the name we give victory in the most decisive battle any man fights — his battle with himself."

A. J. Cronin put it another way: "The virtue of all achievement is victory over oneself. Those who know this victory will never know defeat."

One of my favorite quotes comes from Teddy Roosevelt: "Far better it is to dare mighty things to win glorious triumphs even though checkered by failure, than to rank with those poor spirits who neither enjoy nor suffer much, because they live in that grey twilight that knows neither victory nor defeat." Let's look at each statement in that quote to get the true meaning of what Roosevelt said.

"FAR BETTER IT IS TO DARE MIGHTY THINGS TO WIN GLORIOUS TRIUMPHS"—Roosevelt didn't say "Far better it is to dare ordinary things to win glorious triumphs.'' You can't win glorious triumphs doing ordinary things. It takes courage to dare mighty things. Glorious triumphs, Roosevelt said, should be our goal. Usually in the commercial world, when a person wins glorious triumphs, he get well paid for it. The money is the byproduct of winning glorious triumphs.

"EVEN THOUGH CHECKERED BY FAILURE"—Here Roosevelt advises that those who dare to do *mighty things* will probably experience periodical *failure*. He doesn't say this is bad. He states that periodical failure can be expected. It's a part of the rules of life. Those people who are afraid to fail never try.

"THAN TO RANK WITH THOSE POOR SPIRITS WHO NEVER ENJOY NOR SUFFER MUCH"—Roosevelt says that to win glorious triumphs, a person has to suffer to *enjoy* the fruits of high achievement. We often call this suffering the price we must pay for success—little suffering; little enjoyment.

Valley people suffer the fruits of mediocrity. These include low personal self-esteem, lack of recognition, and not being able to acquire many of the material things in life. Earning a lot of money should not be one's objective, however, in the commercial world the income a person commands is a measure of the value his company places on his services. The weekly paycheck is the score card. Naturally, as a person's income increases, so does his self-esteem.

Personally, I preferred to suffer in order to enjoy the fruits of high achievements—mighty things. Everyone wants the benefits of being able to do *mighty* things, but not to suffer. Many people want to go to heaven, but they don't want to die. They want the benefits of the insurance policy, but they don't want to pay the premiums.

"BECAUSE THEY LIVE IN THAT GREY TWILIGHT THAT KNOWS NEITHER VICTORY NOR DEFEAT"—Roosevelt says that valley people don't win and they don't lose. They don't do much of anything.

An average person takes a job because there was an opening. He or she often works eight hours a day at a job he or she dislikes. Such people dread to see Monday morning come, and they can't wait for Friday afternoon. The man who drives me to the airport doesn't win and doesn't lose. He creates nothing; he betters no one's life; he leads and inspires no one. What a way to spend a life.

If a person accepts Roosevelt's philosophy and the rules for achievement, he is on his way to winning "glorious triumphs."

Lack of Goals

Valley people are not goal-oriented. They are like a ship without a compass. They have given little or no thought to where they will be five years from now.

If you asked me: "How can I get there?" I would ask you: "Do you know where you want to go?" Commitment to goals is essential to success.

All people have personal problems, fears, hangups, complexes, bad habits, and inhibitions. Most of us accommodate these problems rather than try to solve them. Often we use them for excuses for lack of achievement. For instance, timid people say: "I can't sell, I am timid." They say that as if it excuses them for their lack of achivment.

I have supervised managers who say: "I like to sell, but I don't like reports." They hope a company will let them hold a top executive position and not report what they do.

What can one do to begin to achieve victory over one's fears and inhibitions? I believe that each of us should have a rehabilitation program designed to overcome our human frailties. I got ths idea while riding on a train from Chicago to Kansas City in the 1950's. A group of us in the club car were discussing various personalities. One person mentioned a female movie star. A gentleman next to me said she impressed him as being a person with happy emotions. I suspected that he was a psychologist so I asked him about it. He said he wasn't and asked me why I had asked. I told him that describing a movie star as a person with happy emotions appeared to be a statement only a person with that background would make. He said that he had been a patient at the Menninger Clinic in Topeka. He told me of his experience.

When a boy, his alcoholic father would come home drunk and abuse him and his mother. This implanted a sense of insecurity that manifested itself in later years as a lack of ability to make simple decisions. He would wake up in a hotel and smoke three cigarettes beore he got out of bed and underway for the day. He would go to the bathroom and be indecisive about whether to comb his hair or brush his teeth first. He would order eggs and if they were not cooked as he requested, he would not send them back.

He worked as a salesman calling on theatrical people. One morning he woke up in a hotel room in New York City, and went into the bathroom to get a glass of water. He saw a razor blade in the glass and poured out the water. He drew another glass, but the razor blade was still there. He knew he was in trouble, so he contacted the Veterans' Hospital in New York. After preliminary examination, doctors sent him to a hospital affiliated with the Menninger Foundation. The first thing they had him do was read a book. The message in the book was that people are what they are conditioned to be by the early influence of parents, brothers, sisters, church, school, and community. The book helped to relieve him of self-guilt and to realize what caused his problem.

When released from the hospital, doctors gave him a therapeutic rehabilitation program to follow. He was told to never again procrastinate in making a decision. He was to make it, right or wrong, but make it fast. The doctors told him to get out of bed immediately when the alarm rang.

You don't have to be that emotionally incapacitated to profit from that advice. How often have you decided to do something you needed to do, but allowed yourself to do something else? Salespeople do this often. They drive to where they intend to call on a customer. As they approach the customer's home or business, butterflies begin to fly in their stomachs because they fear the prospect may reject them. Instead of making the call, they decide to do something at the office, or they drive home or go to a movie. Every time a person does this he makes himself weaker. His fears get a stronger grip on him.

The solution to this problem is to make a firm commitment to do what you need to do. When you get to the place of business or residence, get out of the car without hesitation and go right to the prospect's door. As you approach that dreaded door, say to yourself: "This prospect needs what I am selling, and he will be better because of owning it. He's going to see me and everything will work out fine."

Humans can make themselves believe anything they want to believe. Medical experts tell us that as much as 85 percent of all physical illness is psychosomatic. Part of the reason is that negative thoughts produce negative actions. But the reverse is also true: positive thoughts produce positive actions. We can choose whether we nourish our minds with positive thoughts that create our successes, or the negative thoughts that defeat us.

Few people consciously screen their thinking. Certainly, the valley people do not.

What Can a Person Do?

Recognizing that we all have problems and that we are our biggest problem, what can a person do to rehabilitate himself? Here are suggestions that will help if practiced regularly.

Never make a decision for immediate gain but long-range loss.

Be honest when evaluating yourself. Humans possess an enormous capacity for self-deception. When you are not honest with yourself, you are the one who is cheated.

Stay away from negative people. They hurt you.

Read about successful people. Identify with successful people.

Read inspirational and self-help books and listen to tapes with inspirational messages. Set aside time each day for this.

Relive your successes, not your failures. Behaviorial scientists say we need periodic positive feedback.

A young, dynamic manager came to my office one day. While he waited for me to complete a phone call, he looked at a yellow piece of paper he obviously had carried with him for a long time. I asked him what was on the page and he handed it to me. At the top was written, "My 35 Victories." There were 35 lines on the page. Several of them were filled in with the dates when he received his college degree, got married, joined our company, and received promotions. He said he always carried the paper and looked at it often. He did this to enhance his self-image. That certainly beats telling yourself how undesirable you are, as some people do.

Never let the sun rise on Monday without a detailed written plan for the week to which you are totally committed.

Set realistic goals and never compromise your commitment to reach them. When you eventually do what you know you should do every week — 52 weeks a year — you will have, as A. J. Cronin said, "Achieved victory over yourself. Those who know this victory will never know defeat." You will stand on the summit of your personal mountain. You will feel good about yourself. You will no longer seek the approval of others, because you will have self-approval.

YOU CAN BE BETTER THAN YOU ARE. I hope those who have read this will never lose the will to be better than they are. You owe it to yourself.

Recommended Books and Tapes

Books

Bettger, Frank, *How I Raised Myself from a Failure to Success in Selling*. New Jersey: Prentice-Hall, 1949.

Blake, R. R., and J. S. Mouton, *Grid for Sales Excellence: Benchmarks for Effective Salesmanship*. New York: McGraw-Hill, 1969.

Collier, Robert, *The Secret of the Ages*. Ramsey, N.J.: Robert Collier Book Corp., n.d.

Hill, Napoleon, *Think and Grow Rich*. New York: Hawthorn, 1966.

Leterman, E. G., *Personal Power Through Creative Selling*. New York: Macmillan, 1962.

Mandino, Og, *The Greatest Miracle in the World*. New York: Frederick Fell, 1975.

————, *The Greatest Salesman in the World*. New York: Frederick Fell, 1968.

————, *The Greatest Secret in the World*. New York: Frederick Fell, 1972.

Mortell, Arthur, *Anatomy of a Successful Salesman*. Rockville Centre, N.Y.: Farnsworth, 1975.

Robert, Cavett, *Success with People Through Human Engineering and Motivation*. Chicago: Success Unlimited, 1976; New York: Frederick Fell, 1977.

Schwartz, David J., *Magic of Self-Direction*. New York: Cornerstone, 1975.

————, *Magic of Thinking Big*. New York: Cornerstone, 1962.

Ziglar, Zig, *See You at the Top*. Louisiana: Pelican, 1974.

There are many other fine books, but those listed here are ones that I have read and have been meaningful to me.

Tapes

Bonnell, Howard W., "Creative Sales Seminar." Chicago: Bonnell; 4-tape album.

————, "You Can Be Better Than You Are." Chicago: Bonnell.

Nightingale, Earl, "Lead the Field." Chicago: Nightingale-Conant; 6-tape album.

————, "The Strangest Secret." Chicago: Nightingale-Conant.

Waitley, Dennis, "The Psychology of Winning." Chicago: Nightingale-Conant; 6-tape album.

INDEX